Seasons of Change

Invoking the Moon and the Magic of the Elements

Based on the live course taught by
MELISSA CORTER and JODIE HARVALA

SEASONS OF CHANGE

Invoking the Moon and the Magic of the Elements

Copyright © 2016. Melissa Corter and Jodie Harvala

All Rights Reserved. No part of this publication may be reproduced, distributed, or transmitted in any form or by any means, including photocopying, recording, or other electronic or mechanical methods, without the prior written permission of the publisher, except in the case of brief quotations embodied in critical reviews and certain other noncommercial uses permitted by copyright law.

Published by

Transcendent Publishing
465 Pinellas Bayway S. #211
Tierra Verde, FL 33715

www.TranscendentPublishing.com

Photography by Melissa Corter

Formatted by Shanda Trofe

ISBN-13: 978-0692673751

ISBN-10: 069267375X

Printed in the United States of America.

CONTENTS

Foreword by Sunny Dawn Johnston..i

Introduction: Jodie Harvala..i

Introduction: Melissa Corter..iii

How Two Magical, Psychic, and Powerful Chicks Came Together..............vii

How to Use this Book x

Acknowledgment & Dedication..ix

Everything Begins with Magic..1

    The Moon and her Magic 1

    2016 Dates of Full & New Moons 2

    During The Moon Phases 2

Season of Winter 11

    The Fire Element 15

    Winter Moon Phases and Dates 22

Season of Spring 33

    The Water Element 36

    Spring Moon Phases and Dates 45

Season of Summer 55

    The Air Element 59

    Summer Moon Phases and Dates 64

Season of Fall/Autumn 75

    Invoking Earth 80

Fall Moon Phases and Dates 84

Thank You 95

Other Products & Services By Melissa Kim Corter 96

Other products & Services by Jodie Harvala 98

RESOURCES 100

FOREWORD BY SUNNY DAWN JOHNSTON

Jodie and Melissa have come together to bring you a fun experience weaving the elements, the moon, and nature together to help you harness them for powerful results in your life. It is always exciting and beautiful when I witness my students become colleagues by creating and putting their passions out into the world, bringing spirit into their messages. As a psychic medium, I recognize the value in supporting the body, mind, and spirit together and believe that earth and nature are just as important to our well-being.

I have had the pleasure of knowing Jodie and Melissa together and individually over the years. They both have unique gifts, and when they come together, they create "magic". By bringing everyday lessons and experiences to you in ways that feel majestic, they open your eyes to the divine that exists in all things and all opportunities. When we come together with focused intention, we can magnify an experience. This is the heart of Jodie & Melissa's work. Throughout the pages of this book, you will feel the differences in their energy and approach, and also witness the harmony that each perspective and teachings creates.

This beautiful guidebook to the elements is a great support tool that will assist you in seeing a new perspective when coming into contact with the elements. Each month, when you feel the changes within, you will begin to learn how the moon's shifts and changes affect your daily life as well. They have even created an exciting experience that takes you on a journey of the seasons, providing you with an opportunity to extract the wisdom each season has to offer, and discover your own wisdom hidden within the elements and the moon.

Each chapter offers you easy to follow exercises to experience each season and element in a deeper way. This book creates an easy pathway to move from the teaching stories to the guided meditations to the beautiful channeled messages within each chapter. The Universe works with us in so many ways and working with the elements, the moon and nature is just another beautiful way for us to harness the amazing and magical energy of spirit.

Listening to spirit is a choice. We each have the opportunity to receive the messages of spirit if we simply open up and listen. Jodie and Melissa have their own unique understanding of guidance and ways of tapping into it which can help you, the reader, gain more insight to your own natural and unique gifts. Connecting to the divine intelligence of your body to discover how you might be affected by weather, the land, the seasons and the pull of the moon can bring greater awareness into your life and help you create a deeper relationship to yourself and your spirit. If you are ready to take the dive within, to discover your connection to nature and the elements, you have the right book in your hands.

Enjoy the journey –

Sunny Dawn Johnston
Best-selling Author of *Invoking the Archangels*, *The Love Never Ends* and *Detox Your Life*
www.sunnydawnjohnston.com

Sunny Dawn Johnston
ANGEL COMMUNICATOR
SPEAKER, TEACHER, PSYCHIC MEDIUM

JODIE HARVALA

Stepping into the magic of spirit has been a road. Sometimes a long road and sometimes a beautiful road and sometimes a crazy road. What I have learned is the more I open up the world, the more the world opens up to me. Because I have a lot of sensitivities to energy I have had to learn to walk through the world a little bit differently. Learning to feel my way through life has been the biggest gift. The elements, the moon and the earth—all parts of this earth—are meant to support us in our journey. Each day we get a choice on how we will walk in the world. With this workbook we wanted to offer you a place to explore and understand how these elements can assist you in your life each and every day! We can't wait to hear about the magic that you create!

~ Jodie Harvala

Jodie Harvala is a forward thinking, spirit loving, space clearing, psychic teacher and coach. She is also the founder of The Spirit School. Walking through her own spirit journey, she went from a fear *based* woman to a Spiritually FearLESS entrepreneur.

Jodie loves teaching others how to connect with spirit and also how to experience spirit in the sacred, everyday moments of life. She teaches through experience. With each and every class offered, people who participate walk away with their own very real experience with spirit and a fresh perspective regarding the next step on their personal journey here on earth.

Jodie shares tools and ideas to connect with spirit on a daily basis, creating your own magical experiences day to day. When we walk through life with direction from spirit, we become fearless. With each course offered at The Spirit School, you will feel more empowered and filled with magic in your own life. Hands on your hearts, ladies and gentleman. It's time to pledge allegiance to your higher self. All aboard the bus to The Spirit School!

www.jodieharvala.com

www.TheSpiritSchool.com

MELISSA CORTER

For many years I struggled with connecting to my body, my environment, and understanding my connection to this earth. Although I spent most of my life in the woods, playing or swimming in the ocean, it took me many moons to recognize how connected my entire life has been to the elements and nature. From a young age I knew there was something very different about how I related to the world around me. I spoke to things that others couldn't see, and treated everything as if it was alive, from the rocks and trees to the grass and sky. There was a magic within it all, a living spirit in everything through my eyes. Along with the earth and her beauty, the moon also pulled me in, her magnificent glow had me mesmerized for as long as I can remember first laying my gaze upon her. Many evenings as a child I recall staring at her through my bedroom window, receiving what felt like messages and stories. Then all of the sudden, during my adolescents I became lost in pre-teen years, my magic and connection to the earth and the moon lessened. At the time in my life I needed it most, the beautiful round glow in the sky was no longer in my awareness. I walked upon the earth carelessly forgetting how she supported my steps, how my tears flowed down into her rivers, and my pain was transformed by the fire burning in my belly. Transitioning from a girl to a woman was chaotic and traumatic, I ignored my body instead of honoring the insight that the moon and her cycles could have guided me through. I did that dance for years before awakening once again to the power and magic the elements and moon always gifted me....and now from this moment I am grateful to once again be navigated by their innate intelligence.

~ Melissa Kim Corter

Melissa Kim Corter is a spiritual teacher. Melissa has discovered the power of helping others reclaim the truth of who they are: a divine spiritual being in a body. Her gifts include sacred sight, a method of using her camera as a tool, and guiding women gently to feel safe and to embrace their divinity. As a certified hypnotherapist and yoga teacher, Melissa also discovered the importance of listening to her spirit and "soul tribe" (her team of guides that help her do her work). She teaches others how to tap into the wisdom that their unique spirit is guiding them to find, so they can share their authenticity with the world.

With over 15 years of experience in everything mind, body, and spirit, Melissa built a holistic practice of clients and students with her unique style and combination of healing modalities and artistic talent. They started coming to her for a unique blending of services including hypnotherapy, spiritual counseling, soul artistry, and shamanism.

Even though her journey began as a photographer looking for beauty in the world, she discovered that everyone is a reflection of each other ... we see in others what we want to see, or are not wanting to see. It then became her intention to see everyone through the eyes and lens of love ... which then unfolded her own journey of learning how to love herself. From me to you: I know what it feels like to stay in the shadows and hide, I lived in that place for many years and it still finds its way into my life when I veer off my path. I have learned that it is safe to be seen and not only is it safe, it is necessary. There are people in this world that need you to show up, trust in that, it is what your spirit has been calling you towards.

www.melissacorter.com

How Two Magical, Psychic, & Powerful Chicks Came Together

I had a big project that I was working on and had called on Melissa for assistance with a few pieces. As soon as we met up that morning, I knew that something for us was coming up. We could both feel this energy and magic and that entire day we spent so much time just chatting and learning and asking questions about each other. I had never met someone that understood the vision in my head as clearly as she did, and as my project came together, the pieces she helped me create fit so perfectly I was blown away. I had heard in my heart that we were meant to work together in some way. When I spoke about the idea she laughed and agreed, and the rest they say is history. Sometimes you ask spirit for certain connections and sometimes it takes a while before they are made. The best part of the two of us is we both bring such different energy to our creations, but for some reason it works together. We do joke that we are the same person at times and I think that is a piece that is the most magical in our time together. She holds those pieces I am still learning about and I do the same for her. We compliment the energy that is presented and we could not wait to create these projects together for the world. We do hope you enjoy every bit of them!

~ Jodie Harvala

I love the synergy and connection I feel working alongside Jodie, we often joke about how we are the same person. We had a project we worked on together for Jodie's business that really started the momentum for our current collaborations. Though we had no idea what we were in store for, this time we spent generated limitless creativity, ideas, and both of us were on fire receiving intuitive messages. We then began chatting and sharing on a regular basis, discovering how much we had in common and also to support each other in an industry that can be very difficult to find people who are with integrity and walking their talk. Bouncing ideas for our separate businesses led to chatting about doing some projects together.

One day Jodie said, "Hey, I'm feeling like we should do something with the moon and the elements". I laughed because I had just got done thinking about pouring more energy into my shamanic aspect and teachings, and was curious thinking of different ways to start that process. This came as no surprise because we both are forever students in the classroom on earth, though we also both have a very deep and special bond with our spirituality and the gifts that come with our lifestyles and backgrounds.

We both trusted spirit to guide us, also having both come off of not so great collaborations in the past, and both wanting to manifest a new experience for ourselves. From the very beginning all the way through, I have no doubt in my mind that spirit was guiding us. There truly has been magic in everything we join forces on and we know that spirit has our backs, working through us to share the messages of our hearts and our individual spirits collectively.

~ Melissa Kim Corter

ACKNOWLEDGMENT & DEDICATION

Thank you to my wonderful family, husband Kristopher and son Jared, for reminding me of my gifts, and sharing me with the world as I pour my energy into another creation. I never take for granted that time is sacred and I appreciate you supporting me in my dreams.

I dedicate this book to all of my soul sisters who are waking up and finding their way, rise up and forge your own path

~ Melissa Kim Corter

Thank you to my boys—always. My husband, Eli, who has always support my life and my work, and my two boys, Foster and Keaton, who each day push me to be a better mom and continue to teach me to play.

I dedicate this book to all those souls who are ready to create magic in life and all the people who support the magic. As we rise up to support each other we all rise up in our own magic and the world needs more magic each and every day!

~ Jodie Harvala

HOW TO USE THIS BOOK

We are believers in absorbing what resonates and leaving the rest behind. Take some time reading through the workbook to get and idea of the flow, then you can come back around and begin in the section of your choice.

Each section is broken down by the season, providing an overview of the energy of the season, stories, teaching lessons, tools, and how to embrace this time for you.

Be ready to dive in and do some work! We have provided various tool and lessons for you to experience as you move through the pages of this workbook. Take your time digging deep, and allowing the experience to move through you. There is always a Full Moon and New Moon in every month, we suggest marking these dates on your calendar as well as the Holy Days to help you track them.

We host a live version of this class a few times per year, visit our website for more information and to register: www.invokingmagic.com. The live class creates connection, provides support, and gives you personal time with Jodie & Melissa.

We would love to have you join us!

EVERYTHING BEGINS WITH MAGIC

Magic. Someone asked me once what was that one thing I wanted to do in my life. I said I wanted a magic wand and I wanted to help people feel better and I wanted to do it with magic. I didn't always know what that magic was. I had been searching for it all my life and had no idea that was what I was searching for. Then I discovered clearing spaces and I will always remember knowing that I had found it. That energy that I had been looking for was right in front of me and I was REMEMBERING how to use it. I knew I had done it in a past life and knew that I would be here to teach others how to do it as well. Magic is that part of you that is true essence of who you are. It's what lights you up and keeps you going when you want to give up. It's that feeling that won't go away. Sometimes it shows up as a sign you just needed to see, a message from a person that you have never met, or even a random tv show or commercial that speaks right to you.

When I was a kid, I remember looking up in the sky on Christmas Eve and saw Santa's sleigh. I KNOW I saw that sleigh and I always tell my children that story and remind them just because others don't see it or believe in your magic it doesn't matter. Our own personal magic is the piece that is so important to hold onto. Let it grow and expand and show that magic to the world. We have all been waiting to see it. If you don't know what your magic is, start asking spirit to show you the magic inside of you. Bring it to surface. Let it shine on friends! How do you know when you have found your magic? It lights you up in small ways or in those big huge ways! It doesn't matter how big or small the magic is the thing to remember is let it in and let it start to grow!

~ Jodie Harvala

I am convinced that I entered into this world with magic in my heart and a fire-filled spirit. Magic was always a word that I would use and more importantly feel. I quickly recognized how it could make others feel uncomfortable, and some believed it to be a childish naivety, a word used for those practicing witchcraft, or illusions conjured up with manipulation. Magic to me was the enchantment of a moment when you witness the harmony of the universe in action, blended with a powerful intention or alchemy of divine spirit meeting the earth in majestical ways. Growing older meant losing a sense of magic for many, yet to me, it was all the more reason to embrace it and summon it into our lives. In a world where so many are stressed out and overworked, we forget to live with the understanding of how each and every one of us is truly a miracle.

My intention is that you invoke the magic that is available to you in every moment and allow spirit to reach you. You can be a responsible adult, parent, or employee, etc. and simultaneously carry the idea that magic exits within all things and lives within every moment. If you struggle with the word magic, replace it with coincidence, synchronicity, divinity, energy, spirit, or anything else you resonate with, whatever you call, summon it into your life and you will then *live* a magical life.

~ Melissa Kim Corter

THE MOON AND HER MAGIC

Her silver light shines so brightly upon me, illuminating the darkened corners of my life, for me to witness and then transform. She has become my ally, my teacher, and my guide. I seek her counsel and follow her pull. As I let go and trust in our connection, life unfolds in magical ways. Struggle dissolves, and plans fall together instead of apart. Life has a harmonious flow just as the tides have their natural rhythm. Thank you, sweet sister moon, for reminding me of my divine connection to the earth, the sky, and the stars.

There are eight phases to the moon: New Moon, Waxing Crescent Moon, Waxing Quarter Moon, Gibbous Moon, Full Moon, Disseminating Moon, Waning Quarter Moon, and Balsamic Moon. We will place more of an emphasis on the New Moon and the Full Moon for this workbook.

~ Melissa Kim Corter

New Moon = New beginnings, a time to plant seeds within the subconscious mind, pour your energy into what you wish to manifest, or bring into form. The next few phases of the moon cycle are the Waxing Moon phases, when the moon grows from nothing into now a slight sliver in the sky, beginning to shine her grace upon us after coming out of the New Moon phase. Waxing moons can be invigorating and exciting. It is a fantastic time to channel your creative energy and go with what you are being called to do, you have lots of energy at this time to support you in projects and creation. The period of the Waxing Moon lasts about 14 days. This was a time that farmers relied on for planting.

From the Waxing Moon cycles of Waxing Crescent Moon and Waxing Quarter Moon, she then moves into the Gibbous Moon, the point of transition from building up to almost full. This is a time to stay focused on the tasks at hand, eliminate your distractions and help projects, ideas, circumstances to take the next steps forward.

Full Moon = Releasing, a time for cleansing, clearing, and letting go. The Full Moon phase is one that most everyone is aware of, usually from the joking of lunatics and crazies out and about. The Full Moon is the time when all of the energy and the building up of the other phases, now moves into completion and begins a process of letting go, or releasing. This is why so many ceremonies are held around the Full Moon. After the Full Moon, the next phases of the disseminating and Waning Moon are about completion, ending of cycles and phases. Transition and release are the themes of this time, imagine the feeling of pulling back, like the tides of the ocean do before the process builds up all over again. The Balsamic Moon is in a way the opposite of the Gibbous Moon as there is more of a sense of urgency to get things done and to move forward. This is a time to tie up loose ends and wrap up projects before beginning anew with the New Moon phase.

The moon frequencies are slightly subtler (intangible) than the subtle-frequencies of our thoughts but are less subtle than the frequencies of the impressions in our mind. The moon frequencies have the capacity to make the thought frequencies from the impressions in our sub-conscious mind to surface to the conscious mind. Once in the conscious mind we become aware of them. Thus one will be influenced as per the predominant impressions in one's mind. (http://www.spiritualresearchfoundation.org/spiritual-problems/effects-of-nature-and-environment/new-full-moon-effects/)

Full Moon names date back to Native Americans, of what is now the northern and eastern United States. The tribes kept track of the seasons by giving distinctive names to each recurring Full Moon. Their names were applied to the entire month in which each occurred. There was some variation in the moon names, but in general, the same ones were current throughout the Algonquin tribes from New England to Lake Superior. European settlers followed that custom and created some of their own names. Since the lunar month is only 29 days long on the average, the Full Moon dates shift from year to year. (from http://farmersalmanac.com/full-moon-names/)

Raven Kaldera says, "The New Moon is the time when you can't see the moon in the sky. It is entirely hidden by the Earth's shadow, but its energy is like that of the seed in the ground, waiting to burst forth. During this phase the moon is often in the same sign as the sun, having circle back around to meet its solar partner once more." (Moon Phases Astrology 2011, pg. 24)

Raven goes on to describe all 12 astrological signs as the stories that all began with the New Moon. He describes the New Moon beautifully when he says, "Everything is just an unformed idea with no manifestation. The archetype here are children and adolescents not yet firm in their own identity but already bearing qualities that will become the basis for what is yet to be." (Moon Phases Astrology 2011, pg. 24)

~ Melissa Kim Corter

"The moon does not fight. It attacks no one. It does not worry. It does not try to crush others. It keeps to its course, but by its very nature, it gently influences. What other body could pull an entire ocean from shore to shore? The moon is faithful to its nature and its power is never diminished."
— Ming-Dao Deng

2016 DATES OF FULL & NEW MOONS

Full Wolf Moon: January 24th – New Moon: Jan. 10th

Full Snow Moon: February 22nd – New Moon: Feb. 8th

Full Worm Moon: March 23rd – New Moon: Mar. 8th

Full Pink Moon: April 22nd – New Moon: Apr. 7th

Full Flower Moon: May 21st – New Moon: May 6th

Full Strawberry Moon: June 20th – New Moon: June 5th

The Full Buck Moon: July 19th – New Moon: July 4th

Full Sturgeon Moon: August 18th – New Moon: Aug. 2nd

Full Corn Moon or Full Harvest Moon: September 16th – New Moon: Sep. 1st

Full Hunter's Moon or Harvest Moon: October 16th – New Moon Oct. 1st & 30th

Full Beaver Moon: November 14th – New Moon Nov. 29th

Full Cold Moon or Full Long Nights Moon: December 14th – New Moon Dec. 29th

DURING THE MOON PHASES

New Moon-Set Goals

Take a few moments to recharge any goals you are working on—or to set new ones. Go back to your journal and spend some time focusing on any goals you would like to work on—whether it be by renewing your energy to reach an existing goal, or allowing ideas for a new goal to come to you. Be gentle with yourself and think about where you can find inspiration for these goals. Once you feel ready, write them down with a focus on renewal and inspiration for the next month.

Meditation: Set intentions to manifest and bring forward the message and action of your spirit at this time.

During the New Moon, focusing attention on action and goals is powerful with the momentum and support you have available during this time and from this particular lunar phase. This meditation encourages a sense of renewal and is more potent during the New Moon. Take some time in solitude where distractions are minimal and find a comfortable spot. Allow your eyes to gently close. Allow thoughts to drift, coming and going from the awareness of your conscious mind. Ask internally or out loud ... what is my next step, and allow those words to become a mantra that you repeat with each breath. After three minutes of asking, then go into silence for five minutes, allowing an answer to surface. Keep in mind, your answer may not come in that moment, but in the hours or days to follow. When you feel complete, thank spirit and allow the eyes to open, feeling charged, energized and excited.

Full Moon-Let Go

The Full Moon is a symbolic time of releasing and creating space in your life by letting go of that which no longer serves you. Find a cozy spot to sit with a journal, or a pen and paper. Make a list of the things you're ready to let go of—guilt, fear, toxic relationships, and negative self-talk. Make a small ceremony out of the letting go process by burning or tearing up the list when you're through with it, either alone or in the company of someone close to you.

Make Space for Deep Rest. Carve out some time to be alone, and ask yourself: How can I deeply rest and recharge during this lunar phase? Follow that inner voice; allow yourself to sleep in, eat comforting and easily digestible foods, read an inspirational book, and practice restorative yoga or yoga nidra.

Meditate. This meditation is perfect anytime you are feeling the need to release and let go in a comfortable and safe manner. Find a space in solitude where distractions are minimal and find a comfortable spot. Allow your eyes to gently close. Allow thoughts to drift, coming and going from the awareness of your conscious mind. Set your intention in this moment to honor your life path and how far you have come. Allow the energy of the Full Moon to surface anything that is ready to be released from your life. Notice any thoughts, feelings, or emotions that come up for you. Sense all of it like water, moving through your experience, and thank it for the lessons it brought to you, and speak to this energy and let it know that you are grateful and it is time to go. Allow the rise and fall of your breath to carry you to the next moment, trusting in the process of letting go. Once you feel complete, imagine now that you are filling yourself back up with light to fill in all the spaces of your life where the released energy once was. Breathe into it and feel the light creating a sense of ease and peace. When ready allow your eyes to float open and carry this experience with you into your day or your dreams.

Moon-Void of Course some believe this is a time to just be, no action, no decisions, or major plans being made. Simply take this time to meditate, go inward and rest. Is also sometimes referred to as a resting phase for the moon.

A Lunar eclipse occurs only during a Full Moon when the moon passes behind the earth into the earth's shadow and the moon, sun, and earth are completely aligned. This process can last for hours whereas a solar eclipse is usually completed within moments.

A Solar Eclipse occurs when the moon moves between the sun and the earth, and appears to block the sun, this can only transpire during a New Moon phase. A total eclipse is when the sun seems to disappear completely by the moon whereas a partial eclipse only blocks a part of the sun.

A Super Moon is either a Full Moon or a New Moon that appears larger because of the distance it is on its orbit in relation to the earth.

The name Super Moon was coined by astrologer Richard Nolle in 1979, who defined a Super Moon as: "...a new or Full moon which occurs with the moon at or near (within 90% of) its closest approach to earth in a given orbit (perigee). In short, earth, moon and sun are all in a line, with moon in its nearest approach to earth."

A Blue Moon is an additional Full Moon that occurs in a month or season when there has already been one Full Moon. It is not blue or a different color, it is just the name given the "extra" moon of this time.

"We ran as if to meet the moon."
—Robert Frost

Altars

Throughout the seasons, we will discuss the importance of having an altar. Altars are a moving energy, they create a vortex of energy that can either feed you, if needed, or assist in clearing your energy, if needed. Think of a fabulous rainbow tornado that is here to help, as it moves energy up into the heavens or brings energy down into your heart. We love the power of altars because they are in constant movement—just like energy is. We can build on them or create a new dynamic with them. They are a sacred space and sometimes those small sacred spaces can be just what your spirit needs to know that it is being given energy and space to grow and expand.

~ Jodie Harvala

The beauty of altars is their diversity in intention, appearance, and energy. Some cultures use altars as a form of worship and honor, while other for the transition of a loved one, or to enhance their prayers. Altars can hold an energetic space for us while inviting that connection to form for manifestation of our prayers and desires.

The first time I really began to understand the power of an altar was long ago when I found myself placing random objects together and then meditating in the space where they would reside. I did not have the language or insight about what an altar was, my spirit simply guided me to create one.

~ Melissa Kim Corter

SEASON OF WINTER

Months: December-February

Element: Fire

"Let us love winter, for it is the spring of genius."

—*Pietro Artino*

The Winter Solstice, also known as Yule, is the shortest day and longest night of the year. It falls on the 21st of December every year. The meaning of the winter solstice is based upon the birth of the sun. The sun is viewed as a physical and spiritual symbol within many cultures. One of my favorite descriptions of the sun and how powerful it can be for us was written in the book, *The Path of the Spiritual Sun*, written by Belsebuub and Angela Pritchard, and states, "The sun that exists in the physical world as the fire we see in the sky also exists in the higher dimension as a spiritual fire, as the spiritual source of creation. This is why there is an overlap in the creation story of Genesis between natural and supernatural phenomenon, and in many accounts of creation in spiritual cultures. The natural phenomenon is the physical, tangible manifestation of the supernatural phenomenon. This is why many spiritual cultures throughout the world venerated the sun, they knew of its supreme, spiritual side."

"The spiritual sun is a living and divine fire, and the highest source of all creation, as explained in the ancient sacred texts from around the world. However, as creation follows universal principles, the birth of the sun also represents the birth of the spiritual sun with an individual in the process of enlightenment. It is born into the time of most darkness- physical sun gives life to the external world; the spiritual sun gives spiritual life to the individual." http://belsebuub.com/articles/the-spiritual-meaning-of-the-winter-solstice.

Winter is now a welcome season in my life. A reminder from nature in the importance of following the natural rhythms of the body. A time for deep introspection, rest, meditation and reflection. The cooling temperatures and icy chill in the air invigorate my lungs and stir my soul. Presence is required of me to decipher the whispers of truth within the briskness of the experience so I am not pulled too far into solitude or isolation.

My body slows down, digesting food and life a little more leisurely. By nature in my regular day to day, I am high energy in short bursts and can easily burn out trying to push through with this type of pace. Winter encourages me to resist the desire to speed through life, energy becoming stored in the body for later, sometimes in the forms of weight gain, procrastination, or fatigue. Days are shorter, the sun seems to move behind the mountains in my Sedona home earlier each day. Conserving energy can feel laborious and challenging when this occurs, the body has its own rhythm and the mind does not always agree with that rhythm.

Though I am very much in tune with my body at this point in my life, I also still struggle from time to time in the winter, rebelling against my body and therefore fighting nature. There is an ease to the season when I honor the gifts it contains. Patience and mindfulness become my guides, reminding me when I wander away from the harmony of the season, my body's needs, and the true state of being within my conscious mind. Meditation becomes the bridge between it all, helping me lessen the thoughts and desire to speed up. Exercise shifts form walking outdoors to gentle yoga or stretching. Movement is important for my body or my thoughts can become stagnant with my body then reflecting this energy back through weight gain. A softer and more sympathetic movement is what is required to balance the need for clearing my body without disrupting the natural rhythms or allowing my ego and mind to re-engage.

~ Melissa Kim Corter

"Thank goodness for the first snow, it was a reminder--no matter how old you became and how much you'd seen, things could still be new if you were willing to believe they still mattered."
— Candace Bushnell

Winter. I live in North Dakota so winter can mean many things. COLD, of course, we can get some pretty harsh temps here. But winter can also mean going within. Quiet. Solitude. It's a time of hibernation for some. I have found over the years I crave winter at times. I have found that at this time in my life I like to get

out and live in it. We like to ski or snowmobile or ice fish. We like to see the fresh snow in the trees and that beauty and silence that only a cold winter day can bring. Have you ever sat in the woods on a winter day? The quiet is different than on a summer day. I watch myself praying for a big blizzard so I can hear that crunch of the snow under my tires and the silence when I pull over in my car just to listen to nothing near the park. It's like an active mediation that gets better with time. Our human mind doesn't take enough quiet time these days. I think that's why winter can be so hard on some people—it means to slow down to re-charge and to go within. Solitude of winter can mean being quiet within your own mind, and that can be a scary place for some people. I invite you to make friends with the silence. The shadows that show up—talk with them, communicate with them and invite them into the light. The winter is a time to lay things to rest that no longer serve you: a pattern, a habit, a belief, a thought pattern—it's OK, let it go. Death is always a sign of re-birth, so allow what no longer serves you to pass so that the rebirth can come to you. We break down so that we may have the breakthrough. Winter can be that support to move into the shadows so that we come out bright in the spring! Each season brings a unique rhythm to it and once you can be mindful of how your body dances with that rhythm, you can then find your own sweet dance at any time of year.

~ Jodie Harvala

THE FIRE ELEMENT

Fire. One of my favorite elements. I am a Leo through and through and the flame and the fire and sound, and even the destruction at times when fire gets out of control, is a force I am pulled towards. I see fire as a place of creation as well, our passion, our spirit heating up as we get closer to who we are. The sun has always been a symbol of healing for me. The heat on my face in the summer days and warming us up on a cold day. Fire can be so transformative. Think about those cold winter days when a fire is burning in the fireplace and the polarities of each one. It's almost as though they totally balance each other out—the freezing cold, the burning flame. Creation at its finest. I also see fire as a way to heal and transform energy. If you have some energy or emotion in your body that doesn't feel good and you're ready to move it and transform it, one of the easiest ways to do that is to journal it out on paper—ground that energy—and burn baby burn! We need to move the energy out to really feel better. Once you have moved it out, it's time to fill yourself back up with a higher vibration. Imagine colored light or a beautiful energy of love filling in all that space you just opened up. Fire can be destructive but in a way of bringing new life. Sometimes it's for our highest good to destruct old ways, burn them down and then build new again. I feel like some people can also get intimidated by that fire inside of them, because at times it's that anger you have inside, and if you were never taught to express that anger in a healthy way it can come up and be explosive and destructive in unhealthy ways. When you can create a friendship with that angry fire, it can honestly change your entire life. It can flame up when needed, but otherwise you have it under control. That exercise above can shift that energy and create a new foundation, so don't be afraid of it. Jump into that fire. Be friends with that fire within. It's part of how we share our light!

~ Jodie Harvala

> *"In the winter she curls up around a good book and dreams away the cold."*
> — *Ben Aaronovitch*

Even as a young child I was always mesmerized by the flickering flames from the candle that was always burning on my kitchen table. It was the most peaceful part of my childhood. When I saw that candle burning, I knew my mother had just cleaned the house and was resting. Fire became this seductive element that you could only get so close to. It was one of my favorite elements for many reasons, and as I grew older I would be the one tending to the fire at the campground and throwing things in to watch them change shape, color, and form. I have a respect for fire and honor it for its ability to shift and also destroy anything in the way. It dances and glows, shedding light to all within its vicinity, warming cold hands and burning away what is ready to be released.

In yoga, the fire element, heat, and the inner fire within each of us is known as tapas. Tapas helps us transform whatever is being called to change. Fire brings transformation, whether you are ready for it or not. Just as a prescribed burn will prevent forest fires and further damage, it gives life to certain plants that need the fire to burn through the seed to release them. New life can spring forward from fire. Sometimes fire creates change that we may not feel quite prepared for, yet our spirit always knows the truth of who we are, and at all times we can handle what is brought to our lives.

Our digestive fire, also known as metabolism, can catapult us forward or keep is stuck in our stories. If any of you have ever worked with the archetypes, then you may be familiar with the spiritual warrior and the victim. The spiritual warrior transforms drama, fear, and problems into lessons, opportunities and growth. The flip side is the archetype of the victim—powerless, uncertain, afraid, not taking responsibility and blaming others or life circumstances for their current reality.

If you allow fire to help you, it can bring you into the space of the spiritual warrior. Embrace your inner fire, allow it to transform all energy that rises up to be honored and then moved out. As you begin and continue to clear out old patterns, habits, and behaviors, it is crucial that you fill yourself back up with love. We need to fill ourselves back up so we do not attract what it was that we just released from our energy and our lives.

~ Melissa Kim Corter

Invoking Fire

"Even the strongest blizzards start with a single snowflake."
— *Sara Raasch*

To call in that energy of fire be open to the whisper of spirit and creative ways to bring fire into your space.

Symbols. At times, just having a picture of fire is enough to get the energy shifting and moving. When sitting in your space, ask yourself if fire needs to be anywhere in your space, and if so, where would be the best place to put a picture or symbol of fire. This is especially helpful if you live in a space where fire is not allowed.

Have you ever heard of that white hot flame? The fire that burns so hot that everything in its path melts and burns up. When you have a deep hurt or emotional trauma, or even just a life long block with a certain part of life that sits in your body, you can call in that white hot flame to burn it away in a gentle and easy manner. Always *always* make sure to fill that space up with a higher vibration of energy.

For Example: I have sadness sitting in my heart.

> *I call upon the element of fire and the white hot flame to assist me in transforming this energy and bringing it back to its original vibration of divine love. In its place I ask the angels to place a rainbow of light and love to fill that space with every color of the rainbow and the emotions of joy, love, laughter, courage, gentleness and creative ways to move forward in my life. And so it is.*

Sometimes our positive vibes and wishes want a little fire energy as well.

I have found these Flying Wish Paper to be really fun when it comes to bringing energy in and allowing that fire energy to assist in the power.

Simply write down your wish and when ready, set your intention. As you light your wish paper on fire, the energy is sent into the universe! Very fun ceremony with a group of people or during the New Moon or even the Full Moon! http://flyingwishpaper.com/

When a loved one passes away, I also love a fire ceremony to honor them. They have the flying wish paper you could use for this or those beautiful fire lamps that you can set into the night with a wish and a prayer for them and for you. I have found it's like writing a letter and getting it sent right to heaven. To watch that flame rise above the earth reminds me they are always watching me from above. It can be very calming and helpful in releasing grief and sadness as well.

When using fire or any element, trust your inner knowing on how to bring that element into play. Spirit is part of each element and is excited to show you how it can serve you best.

~ Jodie Harvala

> *What good is the warmth of summer, without the cold of winter to give it sweetness."*
> *— John Steinbeck*

There are so many wonderful ways for you to invoke the energy and essence of the fire element. You may have an overall intention for invoking fire, yet please remember the strength and destructive nature of this element. It is sacred, and treat it as such when you begin working with fire, and please never leave a burning candle, incense or any other fire item burning when you cannot be in the space to see it ... fire may spread to get your attention. What does the word fire mean to you or bring up in your thoughts? Ask how fire can enhance your life so you may establish a relationship with it.

Call on fire when you:

1. **Want to release old stagnant energy with a burning bowl, fireplace, or fire pit.** You can burn the pages of a journal or your writings.

2. **Decide you want to spice things up in your life.** Fire is a powerful element to move energy, and even just wearing the colors red, orange, or yellow can bring in the element.

3. **Want to transform a situation completely**. If you have an altar you may use fire to help represent space on your altar for transformation.

4. **Want to boost your metabolism.** Fire is the digestive fire within you. Support your body by practicing yoga, going for a walk, and eating spicy foods.

5. **Need a change in life.** Fire can drastically change your life in an instant, ask for the spirit of fire to help you with ease and grace for a change to occur. Use a candle to hold a sacred ceremony for yourself.

6. **Want to create warmth and positivity in your home.** A nice fire in the fireplace is soothing and can create a beautiful ambience in your home.

7. **Want to meditate with a focal point**. Drawing your awareness in and focusing on a flame is a beautiful way to meditate and relax.

8. **Want to take a hot bath to generate some heat and warmth in the body.**

9. **Purify/cleanse the body, mind, or spirit.** Try writing your fears, worries, concerns, or problems then burning them in a fire. Ask for the energy to be transformed as place the papers into the fire.

10. **Want to face your fears.** Ask for fire to transform your fears so you may trust and allow another path to appear before you.

~ Melissa Kim Corter

For Your Winter/Fire Altar

Having an altar for me is actually somewhat new over the last couple years but the longer I have one the more I Learn about what it does for me. It's a place of movement for me. A place for me to focus the energy into a sacred place that offers me a feeling of support and direction that is 100% for *me*. Sometimes we need to hold our dreams close and the altar feels like that sacred place any time I work with it.

I would recommend to ask your spirit how to incorporate that fire element into your altar. Do you need a lot of fire at this time, or less? Keep asking questions to lead you to the answers. Feel your body as you build that altar!

~ Jodie Harvala

For your winter/fire altar, you may want to go in to a meditation, and ask your spirit what fire and the winter months represents to you. Once you can tap into that energy, start pulling together colors, textures, symbols, and sacred items that represent this for you. Keep in mind these few things, an altar is all about helping anchor in the energy in a physical way, meeting spirit in the middle. What can fire help you with at this point in your life? Are you calling for or in need of a transformation? Do you need to move energy? Do you need to change something? How can fire support you in this? How can you embrace the winter season and represent it on your altar? Once you have a better idea of the intention, you can then decide upon the way you want to put together your altar. You may also add the element of fire and season of winter to an altar you already have during that season's timeframe. It does not have to be perfect, or get expensive; you probably have many items around your home at the moment that would already fit perfectly for your altar, yet if you feel guided to purchase something new or different then that can also usher in new energy or experiences for you.

Some of the items you may wish to consider for the element of fire: candles in colors of red, orange, and yellow, anything that supports you in transformation or transmutation of energy. Images of fire, spiritual life force (light). Winter is also a beautiful time for deep inner work, consider sitting near your altar as you meditate, journal, or find solitude during this season.

~ Melissa Kim Corter

"The inner fire is the most important thing mankind possesses"

—Edith Sodergran

WINTER MOON PHASES AND DATES

For the winter months we are transitioning from 2016 to 2017 and begin with a Full Moon in Gemini on December 14th (this is the third Super Moon) and is known as the Cold Moon. The New Moon is on December 29th in the sign of Capricorn

During this month the winter cold fastens its grip, and nights are at their longest and darkest. It is also sometimes called the Moon before Yule. The term Long Night Moon is a doubly appropriate name because the midwinter night is indeed long, and because the moon is above the horizon for a long time. The midwinter Full Moon has a high trajectory across the sky because it is opposite a low Sun. http://farmersalmanac.com/full-moon-names/

2017 is initiated with a Full Moon in Cancer on January 12th also known as the Old Moon. The New Moon in Aquarius is on January 27th.

Amid the cold and deep snows of midwinter, the wolf packs howled hungrily outside Indian villages. Thus, the name for January's Full Moon. Sometimes it was also referred to as the Old Moon, or the Moon After Yule. Some called it the Full Snow Moon, but most tribes applied that name to the next Moon. http://farmersalmanac.com/full-moon-names/

February 10th is the Full Moon in Leo, and the New Moon in Pisces on February 26th.

Since the heaviest snow usually falls during this month, native tribes of the north and east most often called February's Full Moon the Full Snow Moon. Some tribes also referred to this moon as the Full Hunger Moon, since harsh weather conditions in their areas made hunting very difficult. http://farmersalmanac.com/full-moon-names/

In winter we also have two of the Holy Days:

Yule, December 21st (Winter Solstice): This is the Winter Solstice, the shortest day of the year. The festival associated with it celebrates the birth of the new solar year. The solstice is linked to the rebirth and renewal of the sun god, the lord. Associated with Yule is holly, pine, evergreen, tree (Christmas tree), the gods Odin and Pan, cedar, cinnamon, ginger, lemon, orange, sage, rosemary, gold, green, yellow, white, red. The Yule is also known as Day of Children, Midwinter, Mother's Night, Saturnalia, and Christmas. https://carm.org/religious-movements/wicca/wiccan-sabbats-or-holy-days Major Sabbats

Imbolc, February 2nd: Imbolc (imbolg), which means "in milk," is a celebration of fertility and designates the middle of winter. Milk was traditionally poured out upon the ground as a type of offering. Associated with this are the colors white, pink, and red, the amethyst, turquoise, dill, dragon's blood, frankincense, rosemary, and wildflowers. It is also known as Groundhog's Day, Candlemas, Blessing of the Plow, Disting, Feast of the Virgin, Festival of Milk. https://carm.org/religious-movements/wicca/wiccan-sabbats-or-holy-days Major Sabbats

~ Melissa Kim Corter

Lessons of the Season

I remember driving home one winter night. It was about a three hour drive and I was anxious to get home but the roads were slippery and the snow was falling. Driving long distances can be somewhat meditative for me and I remember asking spirit what I needed to know. I had been struggling with several things at that time in my life an felt really overwhelmed and just didn't know how to shift things. I needed a potty break and knew my turn-off was coming up. Instead of becoming a little more present, I let my mind wander and as I took my turn I found myself going *way* too fast and actually screaming out loud and at how fast and out of control I was, going straight into busy traffic. How I stopped and got control back I have no idea. I pulled over and got myself together and took a few minutes to calm down. As I entered the road again, I had slowed down and could breathe again. I heard very clearly to slow down. SLOW down. Why must we always go so fast? Why is it we speed through life? I was always running through life and spirit had just offered me a very scary reminder to slowwww down! We can walk and enjoy and become present. So walk through life, don't run.

~ Jodie Harvala

For many years I dreaded the winter months. For me it was a sign of bitter cold mornings and having to scrape ice of my windshield, and hours wasted shoveling my driveway. It was symbolic of stress and worry because of the gift giving expectations I placed upon myself. There was fear and tons of unnecessary pressure around New Year's resolutions and still not having the perfect body that I wanted or the debt paid off. The cooling temperatures reminded me of the areas in my life that I felt I was failing in.

I was not tuned in and listening to my body at this time, so there was very little awareness around the seasons and how to embrace them. I was very hard on myself and feeling all of the pain and pressure instead of trying to release and create solutions.

Years later, I decided that I will honor how I feel and how the entire situation feels. If I am giving out of obligation, then the person receiving from me is not really receiving me in my heart space, and on some level I believe that is felt. If I give because I feel I have to, I am dishonoring myself and the receiver at the same time. I know this can be a tricky situation since not everyone speaks our lingo or understands how energy works. There will be some transition necessary depending on how comfortable you are holding your boundaries and speaking your truth, and it is worth it!

~ Melissa Kim Corter

A Channeled Message

Dear sweet child,

Release your fear in the deaths of the colder time ... allow the cool grips of the winter months to kill off your self-sabotage and lack. Allow the winter to destroy your self-defeating behaviors, your doubts, worries, and concerns. Allow the fire to burn away the reminiscence that the ego sheds upon you, asking the heavens to regenerate your belief in humanity and your ability to shine through any darkness upon your path. You, my sweet child, are equipped for a million lifetimes of any challenge, any adversity, any opportunity before you.

Drink in the possibility that this moment is nothing less than a catalyst for miracles, the same miracles you have begged for, pleaded to receive ... your miracles await you, fear nothing and give your power away to no one. You have done no wrong, all is well and unfolding for you. The magnitude of prosperity and blessings have been amassing in your favor, patiently anticipating the arrival of your trust, the eyes to witness it, the arms to receive it, and the faith to cultivate it. Let the cold of winter crack open the caverns of your heart, give the burning desire within you permission to torch every ounce of anything less than love. All fear will become love, love for yourself, love for others, and love for mother earth.

You are deeply loved ... beyond the greatest distances, above the heavens, through the galaxies, and into eternity ... the love that exists for you never ends, no beginning, no end.

And so it is.

~ Melissa Kim Corter

Seasonal Homework

Winter can be such an interesting season. Think of the freezing to solid, melting to spring. At times when I have a really frustrating pattern that I keep doing or keep getting challenged with, I will take the issue and write it on a piece of paper and get it a little bit wet and then put it in a freezer bag and freeze it!

Once frozen it feels like it gives me a chance to observe it a bit. A new perspective. I can look at the problem from all sides. Even taking the paper out as it's frozen and turn in around and physically look at it from different perspectives.

As it melts I imagine that challenge melting away from my energy field. Melting into a different form that is easy to dissolve and shift. Its more of a way to physically move energy because it gives your human side something to do while creating that energy clearing that our spirits are looking for.

To end the ceremony, I will oftentimes burn that paper as a way to release it back into 100% light of spirit and divine love! I always notice some kind of shift in the issue and really love the ceremony of the entire process.

~Jodie Harvala

1. Go out into nature and sit quietly. What do you hear? What do you notice about yourself? Do you love the energy of this season, or do you resist it? If so, why?

2. Think about what the animals are doing during this time of year. How are they behaving, what are their habits? How can you learn from their habits?

3. What does this season represent to you? Do you have childhood memories that influence this time of year for you? If so, are there any that need to be recreated or released?

4. How can you honor this season? What is one thing you can do this season to embrace the powerful wisdom that this time holds for you?

5. How can you bring some of what this season has to offer into your home? Are there any recipes, practices, traditions, or celebrations that you could participate in?

JOURNAL

*Use the space provided to reflect on the seasonal homework and record your findings.

_____
_____
_____
_____
_____
_____
_____
_____
_____
_____
_____
_____
_____
_____
_____
_____
_____
_____
_____
_____
_____
_____
_____
_____
_____
_____

Seasonal Meditation

As you start to breath and relax and settle into your physical body you will notice a coolness come over you. Its ok we are just asking spirit to cool those spaces within your body that are ready to be melted and shifted back into divine light. The places in your body that are at a lower vibration that no longer serves you. We take a big breath in as we allow that coolness to fall over us.

We ask that the emotions, the memories, the past life, the stories and pain that no longer serve us are frozen in time, we ask that they gather at our feet, all that coolness moves into our feet from our entire body, and as it gathers we feel that coolness being moved towards mother earth.

As that energy is fully gathered and ready to melt into the earth, we feel that energy melt from our feet into the earth and intend that liquid energy to move into the earth—way down deep into the center of the earth where as it gets closer to the heart of the earth, it starts to heat up again. As that energy hits the heart of the earth, the fire and heat of Mother Earth transforms that energy back into steam and back into oxygen, and that oxygen is turned back into divine live to feed all living beings, plants, animals and humans on earth.

And so it is.

Please feel free to do this as many times as needed when you are working on moving energy out of your body that no longer serves you.

~ Jodie Harvala

JOURNAL

*Use the space provided to reflect on the seasonal meditation. What came up for you?

_____
_____
_____
_____
_____
_____
_____
_____
_____
_____
_____
_____
_____
_____
_____
_____
_____
_____
_____
_____
_____
_____
_____
_____
_____

SEASON OF SPRING

Months: March-May

Element: Water

"Spring has returned. The Earth is like a child that knows poems." ~Rainer Maria Rilke

Spring reminds me of new life, a time to watch the blessings rise from the earth and our hearts, the fertile ground can now bring us evidence of all we have been cultivating within. Spring carries with it a lightness, a clean slate. As the rain falls, we are reminded of the new possibilities that are present in every moment … each breath a chance for clearing the past and opening up to the future.

March is also the time of the Spring Equinox, also known as the Vernal Equinox, when the sun shines directly on the equator and the length of night and day are nearly equal. Equinox means "equal night" and we have two of them in a calendar year, the second falling in the month of September.

A cool breeze emerges among the sweet floral fragrances that caress the air, reminding us that in every moment we can begin anew once more. Spring transitions us from the death of winter to the resurrection of life once again. Many religions, cultures, and sacred teachings throughout the world recognize this time as one where light and dark confront one another, an initiation of sorts moving us from the darkness of winter to the light of spring. Stepping out of the shadows and into the light, dreams have the power to manifest and hearts begin to soften and open. The flicker of the candle becomes a brilliant flame in this time.

There's something about springtime that feels like a breath of new opportunities for all, a fresh slate regardless of who we are and what we've been through.

Another Holy Day of spring is Beltane which falls on April 30th or May 1st. Summer is drawing near, and Beltane brings us through spring into summer. Beltane is sometimes referred to the May-Day festival.

"It is a time when cattle were driven out to the summer pastures. Rituals were performed to protect the cattle, crops and people, and to encourage growth. Special bonfires were kindled, and their flames, smoke and ashes were deemed to have protective powers. The people and their cattle would walk around the bonfire or between two bonfires, and sometimes leap over the flames or embers. All household fires would be doused and then re-lit from the Beltane bonfire. These gatherings would be accompanied by a feast, and some of the food and drink would be offered to the aos sí. Doors, windows, byres and the cattle themselves would be decorated with yellow May flowers, perhaps because they evoked fire."
https://en.wikipedia.org/wiki/Beltane

~ Melisa Kim Corter

> *"No kind action ever stops with itself. One kind action leads to another. Good example is followed. A single act of kindness throws out roots in all directions, and the roots spring up and make new trees. The greatest work that kindness does to others is that it makes them kind themselves."*
> *—Amelia Earhart*

For me spring is a time of renewal, a time of re-birth. When it rains in the spring, I always sigh as it feels like the shower of nature, cleaning all the melted and dirty snow away. I have a funny little saying that between winter and spring we have the season of snit. Snow and shit. I know it's inappropriate but it's true. Spring cleans away the snit and offers a freshly showered path ahead. The air smells clean. The trees start to wake up. The energy in the air is palpable and I love it. I have always considered spring the start to my new year. I love nothing better than driving my car with the radio up as a speed through every puddle in the street. As a kid I loved to jump in them but as an adult I love to speed through them. Think of spring as a time to jump a time to leap forward with your plans. A time where the universe has your back to go ahead and dream a little bigger and see things a little more clearly. To breath deep and allow that new life into your own body and spirit. Spring has sprung and is just waiting for you to spring your new ideas and new directions into the world of spirit so they know what direction to take. Take a breath, face to the sun and shine on friends ... spring has sprung!

~ Jodie Harvala

THE WATER ELEMENT

In many cultures, water was known as the lifeblood that kept them altogether, it is the essence of life. It was a central space that everyone gathered around and for. Water became a crucial ingredient for ceremony, washing clothes, cooking, and bathing. Later, other cultures and religions shifted to using water in their traditions as well, such as baptism, for example, because of the power water has in purification.

Water can connect us to spaces and places within the planet as well as within ourselves that other elements cannot reach. We need water to survive, it's in everything we drink and eat. It symbolizes emotional balance, cleansing the emotional self. Water is alive and has a beautiful spirit of its own. It is said that water has a memory, a way of recalling all of human history. Water, the element that corresponds to winter, points us to that dark, quiet pool within ourselves where our essential self-identity resides. We can use the energy of this season to more deeply discover the essence of our self, and the wisdom of our souls.

Allow emotions to surface and to begin discerning between your emotions and someone else's, especially important for those of us who are empathic.

To work best, water needs to move or flow. Stagnant water breeds rotting things and doesn't fare well in any environment. Water also represents collective intelligence, and imagination. Water will follow the path of least resistance ... where your attention goes, energy flows. Allow water to help you see the areas of your life where your attention and energy are flowing.

I had many experiences before this time, yet this point in my life directed me to pay attention to my "feelings" and spiritual nudges. I was sitting on a log watching a stream of water flow by, when a picture flashed into my mind of me falling into the water. I laughed because it looked so silly in my mind, and didn't make any sense to my little mind at the time. After sitting quietly for about 10 more minutes or so, I went to get up and got my foot caught under some branches, I tripped and fell, falling right into the water the way I had witnessed it happening within my mind's eye. Even at the young age of seven, I was aware that this was more than a knowing, and I was not being punished. I was being given the opportunity to learn how I connect and receive guidance. Water has always been something I have loved to be around my entire life ... until I moved to the desert, then the craving for water seemed to shift. One simple way that I use water is to ground myself. I use water to help me come into the present moment, listen to my body, and to gain clarity. I recommend drinking a glass of water if you feel foggy headed, or need to ground yourself. It is quick and easily accessible without having to worry about where you are or who is watching. For me, water has a direct correlation between my intuition and receiving messages and connecting to my emotional self.

Tips to enhance the energy of water: drink lots of water, cleansing, bathing, standing in the rain, swimming. Allow water to help you wash away what is ready to be released. Water has the potential to reveal to you your deepest emotions.

Just last month, I faced two of my greatest fears, snorkeling and kayaking. Long story short, I had multiple traumatic experiences that involved water, one being the loss of multiple friends in boating accidents, and one time a canoe flipping over as I was trapped and thought I would drown. I am one who believes in facing your fears head on and decided it was time to heal my past traumas. I ended up being on a kayak in the Florida Keys to do a nighttime kayak and paddleboard tour. Water filled into the kayak, it flipped, and next thing I knew I was in the murky nasty water. As soon as my feet hit bottom I panicked and became frantic. All I could think of were creatures coming to get me because we'd seen sharks in the water on the way to where we were. Thankfully no one was hurt and it all worked out. I recognized the power of water in my life and that it had the potential to reach deep within my subconscious mind for old stories that I was ready to release. Had I not gone into the water, I would not have witnessed how I feel out of control and fearful, and what happens when I am in that state of mind, this was truly a gift.

When you tap into the power of the water element you can bring things to the surface that are ready to be healed.

~ Melissa Kim Corter

"Never cut a tree down in the wintertime. Never make a negative decision in the low time. Never make your most important decisions when you are in your worst moods. Wait. Be patient. The storm will pass. The spring will come." ~Robert H. Schuller

Water. When I clear homes, water has always been a symbol of emotion that is needing to be released. I find that if I have a client who is not allowing the emotions to be released and expressed, their home will find a way to do it. A dripping faucet, a broken water heater, a leak in a pipe.

I had a neighbor once who was going overseas for the year. When it was just a couple days away and I could tell the stress was getting to her, I asked her, have you cried yet? Just a good cry to let the stress move out? Nope, no time. Too much to do.

The day they were leaving her washing machine broke and had water all over the place. Growing up I had no idea how to express emotions in a healthy way. I don't know that many parents even know how to teach that piece so I took many classes and courses learning how to express myself in healthier ways. I find that things in my home break down a lot less now. We know crying and expressing and being in a vulnerable place can be very hard for some of you and both Melissa and I honor that. However, we have both learned through our own unfolding of emotions and expression how powerful and strong it really can be. It's an incredible tool in life to have the words and language and tools to express all that water energy.

Water can also be cleansing and/or a conduit for information from spirit or our higher selves. Taking a bath or a shower is sometimes the only thing that can get me unstuck from being in my thoughts and getting me back in my spirit. I can be stuck on a problem with no solution in site and go take a shower and come out knowing the new plan. Sensitive people can use water to help keep our energy fields clean and clear as well. My son used to come home from school in the worst of moods and I would immediately tell him to get into the shower, or we would end up in a power struggle. He would take a shower and actually come out singing and acting like a whole new kid! Today he takes a shower without the fight and for the most part he is in a good mood almost all the time. It's quite amazing the power that water has to clear the energy both inside of us with tears, or even drinking water, or outside exposing ourselves to water.

~ Jodie Harvala

"Sitting quietly, doing nothing, spring comes, and the grass grows by itself"
—*Zen Proverb*

Invoking Water

Water, it flows and pools and moves and spreads and dries up and has many different qualities to it. Water is one of those elements that creates space if we need it. With our tears, each drop helps to move energy. If we are happy, those tears also create space for more happiness. It's an incredibly powerful element that people don't always give enough credit to.

Do you find yourself fighting back tears at times or needing to cry but just won't allow it. The powerful cleanse of water can assist us in so many ways. Think of a stream. As the clear water flows and moves, that is how energy is meant to flow through our bodies. When we stop that movement, we stop the flow. Imagine that pond that has no movement—stagnant, green gross, smells—that is what happens to energy in our body when we don't let that flow move through us. Let the tears fall, let the water move.

On days when the tears are not falling, get yourself into a body of water to allow that energy of movement to work with you. I was told once when I was so stuck in my life to go swimming, to remind myself what it felt like to be in the flow of water. Water reminds us to stay in the flow.

~ Jodie Harvala

There are so many wonderful ways for you to invoke the energy and essence of the water element. As in all things, there can be an overall intention or combination of agreed upon uses, yet find out what the water element means to you personally.

Establish a relationship with it that is your own, the spirit of water will speak to you and provide you with beautiful ways of connection.

Call on water when you:

1. **Need to resolve an emotional issue**. Water can help things rise to the surface of awareness to be transformed and healed. Ask for a gentle and easy process so you feel safe and engaged in the process.

2. **Wish to release pain and suffering.** Ask for the spirit of water to ease your pain, soothe your wounds, and soften your lessons, whether it is emotional or physical pain, it can be healed and you can be supported with comfort.

3. **Want to move through some blocks**. Water is willing to flow through barriers within the mind, limitations from fear, and obstacles along the pathway. Allow water to break the barriers with a visualization as if rushing through and destroying a dam.

4. **Want to establish an emotional connection**. Utilize the power and fluidity of water to sail you to the solutions you are seeking, realize the lessons and gifts of any situation so you can then transform them. Ask water to flow through the heart-center and clear away blockages to opening and connection. Ask water to reveal where you need to "see" more clearly.

5. **Want to forgive yourself or someone else**. Water can heal an aching heart and help wash away resentments. Call on water to help you forgive and release yourself from the anger or resentment.

6. **Want to move some energy.** Water is always best when in motion, you can shower and bath to move energy, visualize and meditate, or swim to move stagnant energy within yourself or as you are dealing with an experience.

7. **Want to increase abundance**. Water flows through all of life and is a great symbol of abundance. It lives within our food, our bodies, and our world to support us. Send love and blessings and image water carrying these blessings to everyone, the planet, and to yourself to open up the flow of abundance in your life.

8. **Want to clear out mental clutter**. Release the clutter of the mind and body by drinking more water and calling on water to release and clear the cutter.

9. **Purify/cleanse the body, mind, or spirit.** Bathing or showering with water and imagining it carrying a beautiful and powerful healing energy to every cell in your body and every particle of thought. Try Himalayan sea salt in your bath to raise the vibration and for a powerful energetic clearing.

10. **Want to increase creativity.** Water can bring us ideas and inspiration, call on the spirit of water to open up to receive and to connect with your spirit.

~ Melissa Kim Corter

"Expect to have hope rekindled. Expect your prayers to be answered in wondrous ways. The dry seasons in life do not last. The spring rains will come again."

—Sarah Ban Breathnach

We wanted to bring to your attention that we can be open to all types of modalities and all types of ceremonies and/or beliefs as we travel this earth. They are all a place of honoring and all our divine right to enjoy and find peace if you feel guided to them.

This particular invocation is actually a blessing that is done over water to create Holy water. The story I have in my own experience of Holy water is quite funny actually. I did not grow up religious but I went to church. I was considered Lutheran so I was not really up to par on my knowledge of Holy water. I ended up doing some energy work on a person with a friend and we had no business working on this woman. We both knew she had some strong energy and that what she was holding onto was something out of our education up to that point. We did it anyway and ended up completely draining our energy and getting what I call energetically slimed. It was ugly. We both looked and felt grey and both jumped on the phone to call our teachers who calmly told us we had no business working on this woman and we had just gotten a college education on not playing in realms we do not fully understand.

It was suggested to me to get Holy water to dowse our space and our bodies with. I stopped to put gasoline in my car and asked the attendant at the store if she was catholic. Kind of, she said. The store was empty. It was just the two of us and that was why I took the time to ask her if she knew where to get any Holy water. From the back of the store the most beautiful man came walking up the aisle. That's the only word I have to describe him. Beautiful. He smiled and said, "If you need Holy water, honey, just go to the big church on Broadway and they will help you!"

"Ok" we both said as he walked out, and I'm not even sure that he bought anything to tell you the truth. We both looked at each other and at the same time said, "Where did *he* come from?" I knew instantly it was an angel.

I found the Holy water through a few embarrassing steps, and as we sprayed the office and ourselves with it we could feel a lifting of energy. We could tell it was working, but most of all we understood that welcoming in other cultures in our spirit work is something that was acceptable and I have since then welcomed in and learned about many new ideas and ceremonies.

~ Jodie Harvala

"Water is the driving force of all nature."

—*Leonardo da Vinci*

For Your Spring/Water Altar

Add a cup, goblet, or chalice to hold space for water, the color blue, fruit or a glass of water. Flowing shapes and symbols, anything that represents the emotional body and the sacral (second) chakra.

When adding the different items to your altar for the energy of water and the season of spring, think of how it makes you feel, and what you would like the altar to represent for you. If spring is a time when you feel lighter, more open and inspired, then add items to your altar that can represent that energy for you. Combine items of appreciation along with items that you are seeking to bring in to your life. If you are utilizing water to bring you more peace or a sense of flow into your life, you might want to add a mini water fountain, or some fresh flowers.

It all comes down to intention. Be mindful of the intention and then build your altar around it. Think of nature and all that blooms and new life that spring brings forward, you can place some seeds or a small plant on your altar.

The sky is the limit as well as your own imagination.

~ Melissa Kim Corter

SPRING MOON PHASES AND DATES

In the time of spring we have a New Moon in Pisces on March 9th and we will experience solar eclipse and a Full Moon in Libra on March 23rd known as the Worm Moon. We will be experiencing a lunar eclipse on this date as well. The Worm Moon according to the Farmer's Almanac states, "As the temperature begins to warm and the ground begins to thaw, earthworm casts appear, heralding the return of the robins. The more northern tribes knew this moon as the Full Crow Moon, when the cawing of crows signaled the end of winter, or the Full Crust Moon, because the snow cover becomes crusted from thawing by day and freezing at night. The Full Sap Moon, marking the time of tapping maple trees, is another variation. To the settlers, it was also known as the Lenten Moon, and was considered to be the last Full Moon of winter."(http://farmersalmanac.com/full-moon-names/)

On April 7th we have the New Moon in Aries and on April 22nd the Full Moon in Scorpio, known as the Pink Moon. The Pink Moon according to the Farmer's Almanac, "This name came from the herb moss pink, or wild ground phlox, which is one of the earliest widespread flowers of the spring. Other names for this month's celestial body include the Full Sprouting Grass Moon, the Egg Moon, and among coastal tribes the Full Fish Moon, because this was the time that the shad swam upstream to spawn. (http://farmersalmanac.com/full-moon-names/)

On May 6th we have the New Moon in Taurus and May 21st the Full Moon in Sagittarius that will also be a Blue Moon known as the Flower Moon. "May, in most areas, flowers are abundant everywhere during this time. Thus, the name of this Moon. Other names include the Full Corn Planting Moon, or the Milk Moon." (http://farmersalmanac.com/full-moon-names/)

Two of the Holy days are during the spring season: The Spring Equinox on March 19th and Beltane on May 1st. Ostara the Spring Equinox is the time of the year when the day and night are of equal length. Ostara is name of the Scandinavian Goddess of spring and the festival deals with fertility, mainly of the animal kingdom and plants. It celebrates the dead of winter and the beginning of the cycle of

Seasons of Change | 45

rebirth. During this festival that was customary to exchange colored eggs. Associated with this festival is moonstone, rose quartz, daffodils, ginger, frankincense, jasmine, nutmeg, sandalwood, rose, blue, pink, and red. It is also known as Alban Eilir, Easter, Lady Day, and Waxing Equinox. (https://carm.org/religious-movements/wicca/wiccan-sabbats-or-holy-days)

Beltane, Occurs on April 30 or May 1 and is the first holiday of summer and signifies the approach of summer and the death of winter. This is an ancient celebration of the return of fertility to the world after it passes through winter. It divided the Celtic year into winter and summer. It stresses human fertility. Associated with this festival is bloodstone, sapphire, frankincense, honeysuckle, jasmine, St. John's Wort, rosemary, green, yellow, and red. It is also known as Beltaine, May Day, Roodmass, and Walpurgis. (https://carm.org/religious-movements/wicca/wiccan-sabbats-or-holy-days)

~ Melissa Kim Corter

Lessons Of The Season

Spring, as much as it feels like new life to me, also can feel a little messy. Even right now I am out in my little "She Shed" office that my husband built for me and my eyes keep falling on messes out in the yard and the neighborhood that were not put away for the winter.

The snow melts and puddles begin. That is where my fun begins as well. I find driving around with the windows open, the sun shining, the radio blasting, and hitting every single puddle I can find the most satisfying way to welcome spring into my space.

My oldest son taught me that sometimes getting a little messy can be fun. He was about two years old and it was finally a warm spring day. We were outside and walking along the sidewalk and he was wearing his tiny rubber boots that he never wanted to take off. All of a sudden he took off running.

Straight into a HUGE puddle that was still half ice and half water. I could feel myself about to yell out to him and tell him to get out of the dirty cold water because he was going to get sick (I am sure your parents told you the same thing- if you get too cold you are going to get sick—OLD untrue story).

All of a sudden he looked at me and his eyes were so big and blue, shining brightly as he was laughing out loud. It caught me by surprise, the unabashed fun he was having. Who was I to stop that fun? I decided right in that moment that it was ok for my child to be dirty and play in the earth. If I was going to be a mom of boys, then I was going to have to learn how to get along with a mess. Little did I know how true that was going to be!

We splashed, I caught a few great pictures, and after a while we were freezing. So we went inside and took a nice hot bubble bath in the middle of the day! Another rule I broke was who took a bath in the middle of the day? I always took baths at night or showers in the morning. It was heaven to break my own rules that I didn't even know I had within myself.

I still catch myself stopping the fun at times and it's something I am learning to go along with instead. Most of the time it's a fear that someone is going to get hurt (fear based living) and 99.9% of the time it's a fake concern. It's just a little fun! SO when those puddles start to form, go get your rubber boots on, jump around, and then take a hot bubble bath and break your own rules!

~ Jodie Harvala

As a child I would spend all of my time outdoors in the spring time, laughing playing, and more often exploring the woods behind my house. I remember once finding a small bunny, hidden underneath a chair that had been left out all winter. The snow was now long gone and signs of spring were everywhere. I wanted to keep the bunny as a pet, yet my parents made me let him go and told me that it would be sad for his parents if he never came back. For some reason though, in my mind, I felt he was abandoned and alone. I felt sad for the little bunny and would cry for days imagining him out there in the world all alone with no one to care for him or keep him safe.

Looking back, I can now recognize the areas of my life where I was not feeling safe or stable in the world. Nature has a beautiful way of operating without question.

The animals, seasons, and elements never question their worth or place in the world, they are just being who and what they are meant to be with the best of their ability. Why, as humans, do we question our value and worth?

Imagine living as if you knew that just merely by breathing and showing up in life everyday, that you are fulfilling your purpose. Could it be possible that all else will be revealed to you as you step forward, letting go of trying and learning to trust in spirit? My spirit decided that my little bunny friend had a beautiful family of support waiting for him, and he was destined to cross my path so I would learn to honor the innate flow within nature.

~ Melissa Kim Corter

A Channeled Message

Dear sweet child,

You have already walked upon the darkest part of your soul, there is nothing for you to fear. All is revealed to you in a perfect harmony, allow the water to surface the hidden pain, and old stories of your life's experiences. Let them float to the surface of your own awareness, allow the sweet soothing presence of your spirit to release them all to Mother Earth.

You are so loved ... embrace the magnificence of the water. Ride the wave of unconditional love through every part of your being. See yourself now floating gently in a sacred pond. With every breath that you take you can feel the space where the water meets your skin, safe within this moment ... sensations, thoughts, and stories passed through you like a gentle breeze, and are easily filtered out into the sacred pond.

Every breath guides you deeper into a state of relaxation, your entire being softening and relaxing into the safety of the water. You feel the water gently pulsating against your skin, and your body, mind, and spirit feeling lighter and lighter. The sacred pond now holds the old stories of your body and your life, easily cleansing and purifying and washing away all that no longer serves you.

Any time you feel resistance to any emotion in your life, call in the element of water. Water is always here and willing to serve you. Allow this element to bring to the surface any and all things that you feel a struggle with or against, ask your spirit to move through the experience like water ... and so it is.

~ Melissa Kim Corter

Seasonal Homework

Water can help wash away our fears and worry. Our sadness and pain. It can help us move energy that is stuck and unable to move on its own. An exercise I love to do is find a body of moving wate, a stream or a river. When feeling like your energy is not able to move and you feel overwhelmed, you can simply pick up a stone that is close to the moving water and hold it close to your heart.

Ask the river or stream if you have permission to throw that stone into the water and ask for help from the water to wash away the energy that is no longer serving you.

Intend for any energy that is bothering you to move into the stone—worry, anger, pressure, fear, sadness—anything that is not of the highest light for you, and as you hold that stone, feel that energy leaving your body and moving into that stone.

When you are ready, throw it with all your might into the river. Feel your body release tension as the water flows over the stone and washes it away.

Do this exercise over and over and over until you feel relief

A couple years ago I did this exercise in Montana at the beautiful Galliton River when I had been feeling a lot of pressure in life. After throwing at least 20 rocks in the river, each one getting bigger and bigger, I ended up having a great laugh with my son and attracting several deer to where our cabin was. It taught me how powerful the energy of water could be in helping me release and open up space in my body to relax and enjoy the vacation.

~ Jodie Harvala

> *"Earth teach me to forget myself as melted snow forgets its life. Earth teach me resignation as the leaves which die in the fall. Earth teach me courage as the tree which stands all alone. Earth teach me regeneration as the seed which rises in the spring."*
> —William Alexander

1. Go out into nature and sit quietly. What do you hear? What do you notice about yourself? Do you love the energy of this season, or do you resist it? If so, why?

2. Think about what the animals are doing during this time of year. How are they behaving, what are their habits? How can you learn from their habits?

3. What does this season represent to you? Do you have childhood memories that influence this time of year for you? If so, are there any that need to be recreated or released?

4. How can you honor this season? What is one thing you can do this season to embrace the powerful wisdom that this time holds for you?

5. How can you bring some of what this season has to offer into your home? Are there any recipes, practices, traditions, or celebrations that you could participate in?

~ Melissa Kim Corter

JOURNAL

*Use the space provided to reflect on the seasonal homework and record your findings.

Seasonal Meditation

God,

Who for the salvation of the human race has built your greatest mysteries upon this substance, in your kindness hear our prayers and pour down the power of your blessing into this element, prepared by many purifications. May this, your creation, be a vessel of divine grace to dispel demons and sicknesses, so that everything that it is sprinkled on in the homes and buildings of the faithful will be rid of all unclean and harmful things. Let no pestilent spirit, no corrupting atmosphere, remain in those places; may all the schemes of the hidden enemy be dispelled. Let whatever might trouble the safety and peace of those who live here be put to flight by this water, so that health, gotten by calling your Holy name, may be made secure against all attacks. Through the Lord, Amen.

~ Jodie Harvala

JOURNAL

*Use the space provided to reflect on the seasonal meditation. What came up for you?

_____
_____
_____
_____
_____
_____
_____
_____
_____

SEASON OF SUMMER

Months: June-August

Element: Air

"Summertime is always the best of what might be."
— *Charles Bowden*

Good times in the summer! When I think of summer I think of the lakes. Here in the Midwest, one of my favorite times of summer is spent at the camper at the lake. As a child, it was my magical getaway, too. I loved to sit on the dock and watch the water for hours. Going fishing was also a favorite activity and still is. I think I like summer because I have such easy access to all the elements. I can enjoy water, the breeze, the bonfire, the earth. I LOVE it. I do believe we love summer at times because we play more. We let our hair down. We don't worry as much. Something about the summer months frees our thinking minds and allows the playful side to come about. The beautiful summer sun heals our body, minds and spirit. The summer sunrise and the summer sunset is also a special time of magic in each day. I hear the animals and the birds and the trees and all the critters coming to life to plan the day.

When my son was tiny, I asked him once if he ever saw fairies. He looked at me and smiled and said, "Yep!" When I asked him to show me where, he suddenly started to point to the lily pads and said THERE and THERE and OVER THERE! He started to laugh and, of course, so did I because though I could not see them, I could feel them playing with him. For me, summer is the time of fairies and magic!

~ Jodie Harvala

> *"Love is like a summer rainstorm in winter.*
> *Where I'm from that's called romance. Where you're from that*
> *may be called snow."*
> *~Jarod Kintz*

As the days now become longer, and the sun shines upon us, there is a vibrancy in the air from the days of summer. The heat builds, sometimes becoming unbearable (especially here in the Southwest). The energy of summer to me feels like a mixture of freedom, beaches and bare toes. I think of the ocean breeze (from where I grew up), family gatherings, staying up late, and having to much to drink. Firepits, camping, howling coyotes, and brilliant starry nights. Summer is a dream, and at the same time, it begins to shift into lazy days with a hope for the breeze to return. Children are excited to be released from the classroom to enjoy two months of play and their own sense of freedom.

I remember being a child a longing for the summer to arrive, and then in the blink of an eye, it was gone ... just like that. This awareness taught me a lot about life, and how our perspectives can shift as we age and decide what is important to us in the moment. Summer never changed, I did, forgetting the magic it contains and the ability it has to rejuvenate and freshen my view of life. Bringing back a beginner's mind, the reminder of joy in the simple things, this is one of the gifts I receive from the summer months.

~ Melissa Kim Corter

The Holy Days of summer include the Midsummer Eve (Summer Solstice), on or around June 21st or 22nd. This is the longest day of the year and celebrates the descent of the sun.

"Most cultures of the Northern Hemisphere mark Midsummer in some ritualized manner and from time immemorial people have acknowledged the rising of the sun on this day. At Stonehenge, the heel-stone marks the midsummer sunrise as seen from the center of the stone circle.

In ancient times, the Summer Solstice was a fire-festival of great importance when the burning of balefires ritually strengthened the sun. It was often marked with torchlight processions, by flaming tar barrels or by wheels bound with straw, which were set alight and rolled down steep hillsides. The Norse especially loved lengthy processions and would gather together their animals, families and lighted torches and parade through the countryside to the celebration site.

The use of fires, as well as providing magical aid to the sun, were also used to drive out evil and to bring fertility and prosperity to men, crops and herds. Blazing gorse or furze was carried around cattle to prevent disease and misfortune; while people would dance around the balefires or leap through the flames as a purifying or strengthening rite. The Celts would light balefires all over their lands from sunset the night before Midsummer until sunset the next day. Around these flames the festivities would take place.

The second Holy Day of summer is Lughnasadh/Lammas on Aug 1. This marks the middle of summer and also marks the beginning of the harvest season.

"This is an Irish Gaelic name for the feast which commemorates the funeral games of Lugh, Celtic god of light, and son of the Sun. In the mythological story of the Wheel of the Year, the Sun God transfers his power into the grain, and is sacrificed when the grain is harvested. So we have a dying, self-sacrificing and resurrecting god of the harvest, who dies for his people so that they may live. Sound familiar?

The power of the sun goes into the grain as it ripens. It is then harvested and made into the first new bread of the season. This is the Saxon hlaef-masse or loaf-mass, now lammas. Seed grain is also saved for planting for next year's crop, so the sun god may be seen to rise again in Spring with the new green shoots, as the sun also rises in the sky. There are many traditions and customs all over the country that are still carried on at harvest-time today.

Lammas is a festival celebrating the first fruits of harvest, the fruits of our labors, and seeing the desires that we had at the start of the year unfold so rituals will be centered around this. Lammas is an early Christian festival, "lammas" means loaf mass and represented the first loaves baked from that years crop. These were taken to church and laid on the altar.

It's a time for bread-making and corn-dollies. Goddesses celebrated around this time include Demeter and Ceres. Trees associated with lammas are Hazel and Gorse and herbs are Sage and Meadowsweet. Colors associated with lammas are golds, yellows and orange for the God and red for the Goddess as mother."

(http://www.thewhitegoddess.co.uk/the_wheel_of_the_year/lammas.asp)

THE AIR ELEMENT

The element of air is present in all of life, sometimes forgotten since it is the less physical and tangible of all the elements. Interestingly enough, without air there would not be life. Breath carries us through our lifetime, it is present and makes itself known, even when we are holding it ... building until it cannot be held any longer. Air is spirit in many forms, reminding us of the unseen yet undoubtedly connected. Prana is another terms for air/wind, and defined as "life force energy", the breath of life, spirit in all. There is no separation within Prana, only the illusion of separation. Everything is one, all are connected. This is the gift of air, the opportunity to heal, connect, release, and thrive all with the breath. Lives are transformed when people discover the power and healing of their breath, learning to control it and allow it to guide them in their lives.

Air is said to connect us to our soul and the breath of life. Air excellent to focus on with anything relating to communication, wisdom or the powers of the mind. It is ideas, knowledge, dreams and wishes. Air is the element of new life and new possibilities and some forms of divination. Air can also assist us in our meditation and visualization if you ask the spirit of air to assist you in letting thoughts pass through. Air is a masculine element and is the vital spirit passing through all things, giving life to all things, moving and filling all things.

The air element can help you carry your desires out into the world, connect more deeply with your spirit, and spirit in general. Communication and thoughts are

Seasons of Change | 59

connected to the air element. When I think of air I feel the power of spirit moving through me, helping me speak the right words, and take the right action. For air, I love to light my favorite incense (Nag Champa) and sit in silence. I am not necessarily trying to meditate or not meditate, but to be present with the moment. I focus on the scent of the incense in the air, sometimes even watching the way the smoke is carried out and fades into the space. Some use a feather, a bell, or even a fan to represent the air element. Choose what works for you and discover how the element of air can help you with your connection to spirit.

Air is movement, and for some too much movement can cause overthinking, worry, or anxiety. If this is the case, try to balance the air element with earth or fire to transform your thoughts. Air carries away your troubles, blows away struggle, and carries positive thoughts to those who are far away. Give your intentions and blessings to air and the wind to be carried into the universe. Air is the manifestation of movement, communication and of the intelligence. As an element, it is invisible, but its reality can be felt in the air that we breathe in every day. To connect with the power of this element, find a place with clean air and breathe deeply, touch a feather or inhale the fragrance of a heavily scented flower. Let yourself experience the energy of this element, and reflect that we also possess air energy within ourselves.

Air truly is the mental element, thought, organization, breath, spinning in mind. I recognized a direct correlation between my thoughts, where I get stuck in my mind and how deeply and slowly I am breathing. During one of the most challenging times of my life, I found the gift of my own breath. I began to slow down my breathing and take in more air, followed by exhaling tension and releasing my worries and fears back into the earth. This process gave me space between my thoughts, which led to more clarity and less anxiety. In turn I was able to make decisions and find peace in experiences that used to terrify me. Utilizing the element of air can help you escape the mental chatter of the mind and re-engage the heart.

> *"Keep your face towards the sunshine and shadows will fall behind you."* —Walt Whitman

Invoking Air

Air is one of my favorite elements to call on when I need assistance or wish to have a deeper connection with spirit. Invoking air is only a thought away, simply seeking to connect is all it takes.

Call on Air when you:

1. **Need to clear your mind of negative self-talk.** This is beneficial for many of us who live in our heads most of the time.

2. **Wish to release pain.** All of the elements can work to release or relieve pain in a variety of ways. I use air to help blow away my headaches and to release pressure in my body.

3. **Want to connect with your spirit.** Air is connected to the wind and the words we hear and say. Ask the spirit of air to bring forward the whispers of your soul to help you form a deeper connection.

4. **Want to communicate more clearly.** Utilize the power and movement of air to send you the words you are seeking, and to speak with integrity and love. Ask the spirit of air to fill your words with the highest vibration so that only love can be felt from you.

5. **Want to feel a universal connection.** Air represent all that fills everything, it is the container and fills the container of life at the same time. Call on air to help you connect to universal wisdom and the Akashic records.

6. **Want to move some energy.** Air can be a powerful element as much as the others. Standing with your arms wide open to receive or to allowing all to be moved through you can be invigorating experience.

7. **Want to increase abundance.** Wind and air can sweep opportunities into your life. Call on air to bring you the resources, people or solutions you need at this time.

8. **Want to calm the mind.** Sometimes you have to empty yourself of stress, anxiety, and energy before it can subside. Call on air to release the thoughts and carry them off to be transformed and to leave your head empty and filled with peace.

9. **Want to send information energetically.** Air is perfect for helping convey messages, speaking to spirit, and passing along information. Use air to transport your message if you are struggling with speaking your truth or talking directly to a particular individual.

10. **If you want to clear your space.** Air is a wonderful element to help clear out a space. Try burning some incense with the intention that the smoke will be carried by the winds of transformation.

For Your Summer/Air Altar

Summer altars can be so fun. I actually used a fire pit last summer for my altar. I took a walk with intention of gathering items from nature to add to my alter. I felt a need for all natural materials and started to gather a whole bunch of fun little trinkets.

I loaded the bottom of the firepit was sand. I used the pit at the lake so the sand seamed fitting as the foundation. I picked rocks and tree branches and items from my walk to create a circle. It felt like a big ole positive vortex and as the time went on that summer and when I would have a hard moment or not feel great I would send that energy into the firepit! At the end of the summer, I did a little ceremony to close it down for the winter. I have full intention of opening it back up at the beginning of each summer to hold space for a beautiful summertime with my family and friends.

~ Jodie Harvala

For your altar, you may add feathers, incense, a fan, circles and other shapes that represent movement and spirit to you. This is a great opportunity for you to allow the air element to carry your messages to loved ones that have passed and let air bring you communication. You can also allow air to help you open up communication. If you need closure or have something to say but do not feel that your words can be understood in this moment, you may place a letter on the altar, asking spirit to help carry out the intention of your message. This is great if there is someone you need to forgive, or someone you need to tell something but you refrain because they may not be able to hear you because of various reasons. Write your letter with everything you wanted to say but never could, let the letter sit on your altar for a few days, then around the Full Moon burn the letter, and ask air to carry the energy into the universe to be completed. Allowing you to feel closure around it.

~ Melissa Kim Corter

SUMMER MOON PHASES AND DATES

On June 5th is a New Moon in Gemini, and June 20th is a Full Moon in Sagittarius. The Full Moon of June is also known as the Strawberry Moon. "This name was universal to every Algonquin tribe. However, in Europe they called it the Rose Moon. Also because the relatively short season for harvesting strawberries comes each year during the month of June, so the Full Moon that occurs during that month was christened for the strawberry!"

July 4th is the New Moon and cancer, and July 19th is a Full Moon in Capricorn; this Full Moon is known as the Buck Moon. "July is normally the month when the new antlers of buck deer push out of their foreheads in coatings of velvety fur. It was also often called the Full Thunder Moon, for the reason that thunderstorms are most frequent during this time. Another name for this month's moon was the Full Hay Moon."

August 2nd is a New Moon in Leo and the Full Moon on August 18th is a lunar eclipse in Aquarius. This Full Moon is known as the Sturgeon Moon. "The fishing tribes are given credit for the naming of this moon, since sturgeon, a large fish of the Great Lakes and other major bodies of water, were most readily caught during this month. A few tribes knew it as the Full Red Moon because, as the moon rises, it appears reddish through any sultry haze. It was also called the Green Corn Moon or Grain Moon." (http://farmersalmanac.com/full-moon-names/)

During the summer months we experience two of the Holy Days:

The Summer Solstice (Midsummer Eve) and Lughnasadh. Midsummer Eve (Summer Solstice), June 21st or 22nd. The longest day of the year and designates a festival of thankfulness. It celebrates the dissent of the sun because too much sun can harm crops. Associated with it are the emerald, jade, tiger's eye, apple, daisy, turn, frankincense, lily, oak, orange, thyme, green, yellow, and white. It is also known as

Litha, Vestalia, and Whitsuntide.

Lughnasadh is on Aug 1, and this festival marks the beginning of the harvest season and the middle of summer. "The word probably derives from the god Lugh, the Celtic Lord of Light. Associated with Lughnasadh is crabapple, ginseng, grapes, potato, berries, green, orange, yellow, and red. It is also known as Ceresalia, First Harvest, Lad Day, and Lammas."

(https://carm.org/religious-movements/wicca/wiccan-sabbats-or-holy-days   Major Sabbats)

Lessons Of The Season

My story is about intuition, Mother Earth and the winds of warning. We had one of those hot summer days and a threat of a summer storm all day. I like to take a bath at night and as I was running my water, I remember having a little sense of not feeling settled in my gut. I looked out the window and saw some storm clouds far away in the distance, so I thought, *oh well, I will still have time to relax a bit in the tub.*

As soon as I climbed into the tub I said, *if I need to get out of the tub, angels, let me know!* I was home alone and was just enjoying some time to just connect to spirit and soak my muscles.

All of a sudden, the wind came up outside the window and I heard, *get out and get out now! Hurry!* As though the wind had carried the message straight into my ears. Of course, this time I listened without hesitation. I hurried and dried off and ran down the stairs to see what was going on. It ended up we had straight line winds and it was taking down tree branches everywhere and the tornado sirens were ringing loud to warn us to get to the basement.

We did not get any damage, except trees coming down, and I was happy to be in the basement instead of a tub of water! The wind will deliver those messages when you ask for its help. That day, I had a shift in my perspective of the wind. These days I love a windy day!

~ Jodie Harvala

One of my most favorite memories of the air element was also one of my saddest. My husband's grandmother had been living with us since we all knew she was living out her final months and would be transitioning soon. She had cancer and at this moment in time unable to get around on her own. One day, I was sitting and talking with her as she lay in her bed. We were talking about life, and for some reason I had a strong sense of urgency to get her in the wheelchair and bring her out onto our tiny little balcony. I asked her if she would be alright with that and she started to beam like a little girl, smiling and excited about the idea. This in itself was a miracle considering that pain she was in, this type of excitement had eluded us all for quite some time.

It took us a long time, yet it was worth every second of that moment to move her from the bed into the chair. As I rolled the chair through the doorway of the patio, everything felt like a different world to me, I felt a shift in the energy around me and she was also changing before my eyes.

She lifted her chin to the sky, closed her eyes and let out a delightful sigh like I had never heard before. She smiled from ear to ear as the sunlight touched her face as if it had never done so before, truly it had been a little while since she had been in the sunshine with everything going on with her health. I smiled just as vast, letting the tears flow down my cheeks. Then as if this moment could not have been more perfect, the wind began to gently blow, moving the last few strands of her waning hair off of her face. I felt her spirit move with the wind, watching her drink in the peace and freedom that this pause of time allowed us to embrace together. Gratitude shot through my heart, bursting it wide open as the tears blurred my vision even further. Together our wishes were different yet the same and her ailing body was now a distant thought in someone else's life experience in this second. The wind moved us both into a new perspective of life ... never were either one of us the same after that moment, and I will always have respect for the wind. The wind whispered the message to me, then allowed us to bask in the beauty of the message together. This was the last time I was able to see the sunlight upon her face before she passed a very short while after, and I will always hold it dear to my heart. Never underestimate the transformation that an element can bring to your doorstep.

~Melissa Kim Corter

A Channeled Message

Deer sweet child,

Allow your body and mind to soften and let go as your absorb these special words. Feel yourself releasing conscious thought, worry, and tension ... melting from the muscles, relaxing, and feeling safe in this experience. Spirit is surrounding you with divine light, you are protected always and in all ways. Your guides and angels are helping you to ease into the energy of receiving your dreams, watching them manifest before you. The deep seated desires of the heart are revealed with ease and trust.

Allow yourself to hand over your wishes, knowing they are in good hands. Let them flow from your spirit into the universe. Continue to breathe, letting go even more. Imagine now, the doors of your heart are opening, opening slowly with every breath, opening wide, so that you may enter, going inward. You feel at peace, trusting in this process, feeling safe and divinely supported. Ask the dreams of your heart to come forward. See a brilliant light flooding your awareness, this light is anchoring your dreams into a higher vibration, allowing them to start moving into form.

Continue to breathe deeply, every breath growing the light brighter and brighter, dreams and hopes becoming more tangible in every moment. Your angels and guides are helping you to pave a way for these dreams to manifest, clearing away the old patterns, habits, and energy of the past.

Receive their blessing, for your highest good, there is nothing for you to do or achieve, simply allow it all to flow into the doors of your heart. The pathway is clear, the road is being paved, all you need to do is believe and allow. Breathe in the possibility, breathe in the love, breathe in the knowing that all is unfolding for you now ... and so it is.

~ Melissa Kim Corter

"I love how summer just wraps its arms around you like a warm blanket." ~Kellie Elmore

Seasonal Homework

When we are at our camper, my sleep schedule is so off but I don't mind. I stay up late and most mornings I am woken up from the early birds noisily chirping away, many times before the sun is even up, so I will get comfy on the couch and watch the sunrise.

The sun sets on the opposite side of the road so many nights I will close my day with a walk to see the sunset. I love it.

This summer, intend that you watch the sun come up and notice how waking up with the sun sets your internal clock to a new rhythm for the day. It's a beautiful time that has that noise of summer but the silence of morning. Ask the sun to be with you all day and invite the healing side of the sun to warm your heart.

At the end of the day, enjoy the ending of the day. A day spent with the rise and set of the sun and you will feel this peacefulness inside your heart like you finally understand what the rhythm of the earth feels like. Why I like doing this is because we all have our own rhythm when we don't have alarms and jobs and kids and all those distractions. A few times a year, I like to reset my rhythm with the sun and shortly after can start to feel my own rhythm again.

You can also do this with the moon. It's a different energy but just as magical!

~ Jodie Harvala

"It's a smile, it's a kiss, it's a sip of wine ... it's summertime!"
— Kenny Chesney

Go out into nature and sit quietly. What do you hear? What do you notice about yourself? Do you love the energy of this season, or do you resist it? If so, why?

Think about what the animals are doing during this time of year. How are they behaving, what are their habits? How can you learn from their habits?

What does this season represent to you? Do you have childhood memories that influence this time of year for you? If so, are there any that need to be recreated or released?

How can you honor this season? What is one thing you can do this season to embrace the powerful wisdom that this time holds for you?

How can you bring some of what this season has to offer into your home? Are there any recipes, practices, traditions, or celebrations that you could participate in?

~ Melissa Kim Corter

JOURNAL

*Use the space provided to reflect on the seasonal homework and record your findings.

Seasonal Meditation

Let's all take a deep breath together, allow your body and mind to soften and let go. Feel yourself releasing conscious thought, worry, and tension ... melting from the muscles, relaxing, and feeling safe in this experience.

Spirit is surrounding you with divine light, you are protected always and in all ways. Your guides and angels are helping you to ease into the energy of receiving your dreams, watching them manifest before you. The deep seated desires of the heart are revealed with ease and trust. Allow yourself to hand over your wishes, knowing they are in good hands. Let the air and wind carry them from your spirit into the universe. Continue to breathe, letting go even more. Feeling the depth of the air in your lungs, taking a moment to have gratitude from this experience, as breath means life.

Imagine now, the doors of your heart are opening, opening slowly with every breath, opening wide, so that you may enter, going inward. You feel at peace, trusting in this process, feeling safe and divinely supported. Ask the dreams of your heart to come forward. See a brilliant light flooding your awareness, this light is anchoring your dreams into a higher vibration, allowing them to start moving into form. You continue to breathe deeply, every breath growing the light brighter and brighter, dreams and hopes becoming more tangible in every moment. Your angels and guides are helping you to pave a way for these dreams to manifest, clearing away the old patterns, habits, and energy of the past.

Receive their blessing, for your highest good, there is nothing for you to do or achieve, simply allow it all to flow into the doors of your heart. The pathway is clear, the road is being paved, all you need to do is believe and allow. Breathe in the possibility, breathe in the love, breathe in the knowing that all is unfolding for you now ... and so it is.

When you are ready, allow your eyes to gently float open.

~ Melissa Kim Corter

JOURNAL

*Use the space provided to reflect on the seasonal meditation. What came up for you?

_____

SEASON OF FALL/AUTUMN

Months: September–November

Element: Earth

"The tints of autumn...a mighty flower garden blossoming under the spell of the enchanter, frost."

~John Greenleaf Whittier

Seasons of Change | 75

Fall, my favorite season of them all. The sweet smell of cinnamon and vanilla chai wafts the air as leaves plummet representing the colors of a rich sunset. Red, brown, gold, and yellow in infinite waves sweep the streets and line countless yards. There is a briskness in the air that softy call our attention to evenings getting cooler and days becoming shorter.

As a child, I loved the summer and as an adult it is the season of fall. A time of wrapping up projects before the hectic holiday mania sets in. There is a slight sense of urgency, yet it is overshadowed by gratitude and the onset of family gatherings.

The streets slow down, to be replaced with the crunching of leaves underfoot. The landscape reminds us once again of how magnificent her transformation really is as it happens before our eyes in a myriad of colors and textures. I sit in silence, taking it all in, my meditations feel more powerful during autumn and fall. I resonate so deeply with the earth and these next few months almost as if mother earth is nodding in approval and recognition of my connection and appreciation to her.

We have two more Holy Days at this time:

Mabon, the Autumn Equinox, is on or around Sept 21 and is a time of harvest when the day and night are of equal length. The autumnal equinox occurs when the sun crosses the equator on its apparent journey southward, and we experience a day and a night that are of equal duration. Up until Mabon, the hours of daylight have been greater than the hours from dusk to dawn. But from now on, the reverse holds true, and for the moment nature is in balance. It is a time to reap what you have sown, of giving thanks for the harvest and the bounty the Earth provides. For finishing up old projects and plans and planting the seeds for new enterprises or a change in lifestyle. Mabon is a time of celebration and balance.

This is the time to look back, not just on the past year, but also your life, and to plan for the future. In the rhythm of the year, Mabon is a time of rest and celebration, after the hard work of gathering the crops. Warm autumn days are followed by chill nights, as the Old Sun God returns to the embrace of the Goddess. The passing of Mabon is inevitable and The Sun God should be mourned. We too, must remember that all things must come to an end. So the Sun God journeys into the lands of winter and into the Goddess' loving arms, but endings are a good time to celebrate our successes, thank our selves and those who helped us, and take part in the balance of life!" http://www.thewhitegoddess.co.uk/the_wheel_of_the_year/mabon_-_autumn_equinox.asp

The second Holy day of the autumn/fall season is Samhain on Oct 31.

"Samhain (Summer's End) is one of our four Greater Sabbats, the highest Holy day of witches. It is a cross quarter day, situated between Autumn Equinox and Winter Solstice. Samhain is a major festival with several aspects. It is new year's eve for witches, as well as our third and final harvest festival. Samhain inaugurates Winter, is the final chance to dry herbs for winter storage, and a night when fairies supposedly afoot working mischief. It is also the Day of the Dead for us as it was for the Celts, Egyptians and ancient Mexicans, the night when we remember our loved ones and honour our ancestors. We also celebrate reincarnation and note the absence the Sun (the god), who will be reborn at Winter Solstice as the Child of Promise. Astrologically, Samhain marks the rising of the Pleiades."

http://www.thewhitegoddess.co.uk/the_wheel_of_the_year/samhain.asp

~ Melissa Kim Corter

> *"Fall has always been my favorite season. The time when everything bursts with its last beauty, as if nature had been saving up all year for the grand finale."*
> *— Lauren DeStefano*

The Earth Element

Just writing about the earth makes me feel better. Feeling the ground under my feet, a stable place to rest and feel grounded. The earth always has called to me. I clear a lot of spaces and one of the things I am always brought to is the earth and the area around the space. Sending Earth love and receiving that energy back is one of my favorite feelings. A lot of people think the Earth is unhealthy and getting worse as time goes on but I really do believe it's the opposite. We are becoming more mindful of all the pollution and things we do to hurt her and these new generations will be called to heal her. That is the way of the world. We find ways to heal our wounds including Mother Earth. As we heal, she heals, and she heals, we heal.

When you sit upon the earth, feel the energy coming through your body. When you need to feel that unconditional love, allow mother earth to reach out and hold you.

~ Jodie Harvala

"Winter is an etching, Spring a watercolor, Summer an oil painting, and autumn a mosaic of them all."

—Stanley Horowitz

Also known as Grandmother Earth, many native cultures honored her as a conscious being, alive and responsible for watching over all living beings and creatures.

Earth can be very healing, and with all of the elements there should be a level of reverence and respect. Just as earth can support us, we can also feel our foundation sinking or shaking when we challenge the earth element and the lessons that are ready to be revealed to us. For those of you who study the chakras, the seven energetic centers of the body, the earth is connected to the first three chakras, helping us to ground and also manifest things into being. We are comprised of matter, a density that it considered earth, and when the time comes and we make our transition to spirit, we will leave behind our earthy matter to be transformed. I have healed a variety of areas of my life by calling upon Grandmother Earth and embracing her energy. I am continuously in awe of how the elements support me in my journey of healing.

Earth has always been the element that I come to when I am in need of healing, compassion for myself and others, or to feel rejuvenated. Nothing reminds me of my connection to this physical plane more than planting my feet in the dirt, hiking through the woods, or sitting in nature. For a long time, I lived in a city area and felt like I was living someone else's life for many years. Once I moved into the woods, I discovered how much my body and spirit craves this type of environment. There came a time when visiting nature and the woods on a monthly basis was just not enough ... I needed to wake up there, be in it every day. One of my favorite ways of connecting with earth energy is to go out into nature and find a space where you can put your bare feet on the soil. Pick the soil up with your hands, and if it feels right gently inhale the scent of the soil (you do not have to hold it close for this).

~ Melissa Kim Corter

Autumn is a second spring when every leaf is a flower.
— *Albert Camus*

Invoking Earth

When my youngest son was just a couple years old I took him to the park. We had one of those tough days that day and that evening we just needed to get out of the house and some space from each other. Happily, we lived close to the park and walked over to let the kids run for a while.

My youngest took off over to the monkey bars. He was too little to do them but he had other plans anyways. I watched him run over the little tiny rocks and lie down in those rocks and for the next 15 minutes he took handfuls of rocks and put them over his whole entire body. (This was one of those mom moments when I almost told him to stop but my spirit said keep watching!)

I watched as his energy that had been spikey and crabby all day became calm and serene in a matter of minutes. He was grounding himself with the rocks as he was on the earth and loving every second of it.

After a few minutes I told my older son if it's working for him maybe it will work for us so the three of sat in those rock and let them slide over us and into our hands and we held them and sat quietly and just let the earth calm and ground us. We had a nice and quiet night that night and I will never forget the knowledge that my two-year-old passed on to me that day. (Have I mentioned how smart children are if we let them teach us?)

~Jodie Harvala

Earth is the element I call on immediately when I am feeling scattered, fearful, or anxious. I am definitely an earthy girl, no surprise to anyone who knows me, and it is because I feel so connected to the earth that it shows in all that I do.

Call on Earth when you:

1. **Need to release other people's stuff.** So many of us are empaths and do not even know it, we tend to carry baggage of others. Earth can help absorb and transform this energy for you.

2. **Wish to release pain.** Like mentioned before, all elements can shift or release pain. I use earth when I have more mental or emotional pain then physical, yet it can be used for any of the above, it relies on your belief in it. Sit on the ground or near and tree and allow the earth to take it away for you.

3. **Want to connect to the earthly realm and its beautiful creatures.** Earth can help transport you deep within yourself and other worlds. Call on earth to gain clarity on the guidance from animal messengers.

4. **Want to manifest physical items.** Earth is also connected to the root chakra, and this is one of the lower chakras that is tied to brining items into physical form. Use earth to imagine bringing items down from spirit into your life.

5. **Want to bring ideas to life.** Many of us get stuck in a cycle of having tons of ideas without the action to back it all up. Call on earth to help you focus and concentrate while manifesting all that you need to produce a result from your idea.

6. **Want to move some energy.** Just like the other elements, earth can move energy and be a stable or solid form of what you also want to bring in. Think of your entire altar as earth, holding space as a physical form for you to anchor into.

7. **Want to increase abundance.** Call on earth to move energy down from the head (6th and 7th chakras) into form (the root chakra). Ceremony to honor the earth and you need for material (not in excess) items while you walk this planet because that is the form of exchange we currently honor.

8. **Want to help your body.** Earth represent the physical body, the density of our form. Earth can help you discern the messages your body is trying to teach you if you learn how to listen to it.

9. **Want to heal past life karma.** Calling on earth to release ties, binds, and connections to anyone or situations from the past that are affecting you today.

10. **Want to honor your ancestors.** Call on earth to help you gain an understanding of the messages, insight, and guidance that loved ones here and gone are trying to help you recognize.

~ Melissa Kim Corter

"Love the trees until their leaves fall off, then encourage them to try again next year."

~Chad Sugg

For Your Fall/Earth Altar

As we have discussed through the various section, altars are a wonderful way to open up an energetic space to help you create change in your life. For my earth altar I used a brown scarf, the deity Ganesha because he is known as the remover of obstacles. I add Ganesha to my altars to help remove obstacles to my truth, my spirit, and to clearly receive the messages from the land and its animal spirits. You can use a deity, angels, gods, mentor, teachers, or anyone you feel drawn to receive help from. It does not matter if there are here in the physical realm or have passed. I placed a heart stone from Boyton Canyon vortex from here is Sedona, Arizona, a spirit stick I made with materials that came from the earth, and a

Mala for trust in spirit to guide me. I also have a Bees wax candle for another connection to the earth energy. I have a salt lamp on my altar & a crystal in the center to represent earth spirit keeper of the altar.

To represent the fall season and the earth element, you can use almost any physical object that is dense, and can hold space. Place stones, leaves, or a cup of soil on your altar. Fall is allowing the natural process of death to unfold, so an altar for transition can also be a wonderful way to honor the seasons. Many people in various cultures use altars to honor loved ones that have passed on or are leaving the earth.

~ Melissa Kim Corter

For me the earth altar is all about anything you can find sitting on the ground.

Leaves, tree branches, seeds, pinecones, rocks, stones, feathers, sand or even plain old dirt. I love living plants for my earth altar. From the earth comes life so I try to use anything that is reminding me to live this life I have been given. What gives me the energy of earth. That is the energy I use for my earth altars.

~ Jodie Harvala

> *"You carry Mother Earth within you. She is not outside of you. Mother Earth is not just your environment. In that insight of inter-being, it is possible to have real communication with the Earth, which is the highest form of prayer."*
>
> *—Thich Nhat Hanh*

FALL MOON PHASES AND DATES

The New Moon on September 1st is a solar eclipse in the sign of Virgo and on September 16th the Full Moon is a lunar eclipse in Pisces. This Full Moon is known as the Harvest Moon or the Corn Moon.

"This Full Moon's name is attributed to Native Americans because it marked when corn was supposed to be harvested. Most often, the September Full Moon is actually the Harvest Moon, which is the Full Moon that occurs closest to the autumn equinox. In two years out of three, the Harvest Moon comes in September, but in some years it occurs in October. At the peak of harvest, farmers can work late into the night by the light of this moon. Usually the Full Moon rises an average of 50 minutes later each night, but for the few nights around the Harvest Moon, the moon seems to rise at nearly the same time each night: just 25 to 30 minutes later across the U.S., and only 10 to 20 minutes later for much of Canada and Europe. Corn, pumpkins, squash, beans, and wild rice the chief Indian staples are now ready for gathering." http://farmersalmanac.com/full-moon-names/

October 1st is a New Moon in Libra and October 16th is a Full Moon in Aries and the first Super Moon of the year. This Full Moon is known as the Hunter's Moon or Harvest Moon. October 30 is a New Moon in Scorpio and at the Black Moon. "This Full Moon is often referred to as the Full Hunter's Moon, Blood Moon, or Sanguine Moon. Many moons ago, Native Americans named this bright moon for obvious reasons. The leaves are falling from trees, the deer are fattened, and it's time to begin storing up meat for the long winter ahead. Because the fields were traditionally reaped in late September or early October, hunters could easily see fox and other animals that come out to glean from the fallen grains. Probably because of the threat of winter looming close, the Hunter's Moon is generally accorded with special honor, historically serving as an important feast day in both Western Europe and among many Native American tribes." http://farmersalmanac.com/full-moon-names/

November 14th is a Full Moon in Taurus and the second Super Moon, and November 29th is a New Moon in Sagittarius. "This was the time to set beaver traps before the swamps froze, to ensure a supply of warm winter furs. Another interpretation suggests that the name Full Beaver Moon comes from the fact that the beavers are now actively preparing for winter. It is sometimes also referred to as the Frosty Moon." (http://farmersalmanac.com/full-moon-names/)

The two Holy Days of Autumn/Fall are the Autumn Equinox and Samhain:

Mabon, Autumn Equinox, Sept 21. The day and night are of equal length, and his is a festival that designates the beginning of fall. It marks the dissent of the Goddess into the underworld. Associated with it are amethyst, topaz, acorns, corn, frankincense, great, oak, wheat, brown, and orange. It is also known as Mabon, Alban Elfer, Harcest, Second, Harvest, and Wine Harvest. (https://carm.org/religious-movements/wicca/wiccan-sabbats-or-holy-days Major Sabbats)

Samhain is on October 31 and means "summer's end" and marks the beginning of winter. "For most Wiccans, this is the new year anytime of reflection where the oldest let go and the new is anticipated. From ancient times it designates the end of the harvest season. Associated with the festival are the colors black and orange, obsidian, Onyx, apples, catnip, corn, pears, squash, and wormwood. It is also known as Halloween, All Hallows Eve, Blood feast, Celtic New Year, Day of the Dead, Last Harvest, Winters Eve, etc." (https://carm.org/religious-movements/wicca/wiccan-sabbats-or-holy-days-Major Sabbats)

~ Melissa Kim Corter

LESSONS OF THE SEASON

I was working with a coach, Devon Combs www.Beyondthearena.com, last year because I knew I had some big shift coming in my business and I was not quite sure how to make it all happen.

I had some emotional blocks as well and so we wanted to start with that first.

She had me do the coolest exercise that I have never forgotten.

I had been parked down by the park and she told me to get out of my car.

Pick a tree anywhere in the park that I was drawn to.

I picked this tree and she asked me to explain what I was feeling and why I picked that tree.

It was strong, it had a lot of branches, and it looked a little more flexible then other trees. She told me to keep telling her what I saw.

All of sudden I could see that tree was surrounded by a circle of trees. It had this circle of support around it, and if you would not have paused, you would have never noticed it.

I saw the river behind the tree and reminding it that we always have movement around us.

I saw a ton of little animals running in and out like they had certain little jobs to do.

I saw the tree was healthy and ready to grow.

All of a sudden it dawns on me that this tree is ME. I was seeing the support I didn't think I had I was seeing that energy was moving all around because energy always moves and I was seeing how strong and healthy and ready to grow.

I LOVED it.

I still will use this exercise when I am stuck or challenged with something.

I simply pick a tree I am guided to and keep asking myself what else do I see? What else do I see? This always gives me a new perspective on how to move forward!

~ Jodie Harvala

Halloween has always been a "holiday" that I loved, from as far back as I could remember. One Halloween in particular, I recall wearing my costume, running excitedly from house to house. I cannot recall my age aside from knowing I was old enough to not have my parents at my side.

All of the sudden, hidden underneath the weight of my costume and the plastic of my mask, I felt different. I felt safe, completely relaxed and started to act or "take on" what I thought was the energy of my character. I walked a little taller, laughed a little harder, and was outgoing and joyful bouncing from house to house playing out this new role.

Hours of fun commenced until achy feet and disappearing porch lights signaled that the evening was coming to an end. Like magic, as soon as my cape and mask were removed I shifted back to my regular, quiet, insecure self. It was almost like another person had borrowed my body for an evening to run around and be free. It took me many years to recognize the gift and lesson of this experience and why I was so excited for Halloween every year. I was allowed to be someone other than the person I knew.

Now, as an adult and many years of self-work and discovery, I know the truth of who I am and that I can show up however I choose in any given moment ... without the cape and mask.

~ Melissa Kim Corter

A Channeled Message

Dear sweet child,

The time is now to release the roots of fear. You were always safe ... even during your most difficult life experiences. The "story" was merely the channel for you to receive a lesson that served your personal growth. The process has already begun, allow it to unfold, there is no thing that can replace your inner compass. Take part in the classes, workshops, you never stop learning and seeking ... just be mindful of when you are avoiding being the teacher to perpetuate the pattern of self-sabotage. All this means is that you have not yet fully trusted in your spiritual gifts.

Take a salt bath, clear your energy, and do a burn release ceremony to shift into where you are ready to reside in this time and space. It is safe to put your roots down, it is no longer the time to be on the go. You know what the next step is, stop saying "I don't know" you do, you do hear your spirit, your guides, and you can trust in the guidance you are receiving. Do not fear to uncover the layers, you will not ever be shocked by what you find, only a simple recognition of the truth you already felt. You are safe and all you have experienced was perfectly divine.

And so it is...

~ Melissa Kim Corter

Seasonal Homework

For me, walks in the fall with the woods is the best sound ever. Those leaves crunching under my feet and the smell of the trees and everything around me getting ready to quiet down for winter. I love it.

Walk every day outside. Feel the leaves under your feet.

Create a new routine that in each season a daily or even weekly walk is in order. Each season has its own special magic. Our job is to enjoy it.

Walking into the trees, I would advise you to learn to touch the trees gently and ask if you can feel the heartbeat. If you have never done so It's a totally magical feeling. And typically unexpected!

Feel the heartbeat of a tree is like feeling your own life. Trees have life, they have stories, they are here to share with us and allow us to gain knowledge from them. Go talk to trees this fall and see what it is they have to teach you!

~ Jodie Harvala

Go out into nature and sit quietly, what do you hear? What do you notice about yourself? Do you love the energy of this season, or do you resist it? If so, why?

Think about what the animals are doing during this time of year. How are they behaving, what are their habits? How can you learn from their habits?

What does this season represent to you? Do you have childhood memories that influence this time of year for you? If so are there any that need to be recreated or released?

How can you honor this season? What is one thing you can do this season to embrace the powerful wisdom that this time holds for you?

How can you bring some of what this season has to offer into your home? Are there any recipes, practices, traditions, or celebrations that you could participate in?

~ Melissa Kim Corter

"Autumn is a second spring when every leaf is a flower."

—*Albert Camus*

JOURNAL

*Use the space provided to reflect on the seasonal homework and record your findings.

_____
_____
_____
_____
_____
_____
_____
_____
_____
_____
_____
_____
_____
_____
_____
_____
_____
_____
_____
_____
_____
_____
_____

Seasonal Meditation

As you take a nice big breath, use your imagination that you are a huge beautiful Oak tree. You are tall and strong and beautiful with a huge amount of leaves that adorn every branch.

As you think about fall and what it means for the season to come to an end, I want you to watch the leaves of each branch start to turn and change colors.

As each leave turns and shifts to a new color of fall, I want you to know that is what happens to us every year. Each piece of us grows and expands. Our bodies change. Our cells change. Our thoughts change. We grow and expand and we must make room for that newness that is always within us. So we must let go of the old to make room for the new.

Imagine watching those beautiful leaves changing colors to signify that you have grown and changed and are ready to make room for more of who you really are. You are ready to let go of all that no longer serves you.

You are ready to let those leaves drop into the earth. As the leaves drop you will feel your physical, mental and emotional body become lighter and lighter and a sense of space opening up inside of yourself. You will feel those old pieces that no longer serve you drop away easily and gracefully.

Some of you may need a gust of wind to come up to remove all the leaves. Some of you may want to watch each and every one drop silently and quietly. We never are wrong when doing a active meditation to release energy.

As all the leaves move into the earth, we intend and trust they will go back into the earth to be gifted back to us as divine love and light when it is time for us to don our new selves in the spring. After we shed the old the new comes forward as big beautiful green leaves of fresh and new life. The little buds of life turning into a beautiful green tree full of life and ready for the next circle of life.

Each fall let those leaves fall with ease and grace. We have no use to hold onto the old. We are here to evolve forward with a fresh start at all times.

And so it is.

~ Jodie Harvala

JOURNAL

*Use the space provided to reflect on the seasonal mediation. What came up for you?

_____
_____
_____
_____
_____
_____
_____
_____
_____
_____
_____
_____
_____
_____
_____
_____
_____
_____
_____
_____
_____
_____
_____
_____
_____

THANK YOU

I want thank all of you that took part in this journey with us. Creating the program and this workbook has been incredibly eye opening and spirit-led for both of us and as I sit here and finish up with this last paragraph, I know it's just the beginning of our work together in whatever way that looks. My wish for you is that you always honor the earth and the elements in a way that honors your journey. Some days you may be totally connected and some days not as much, but I feel like they pull at us when it's time for us to work with them again and again. In gratitude to all the people that took part in our programs and all the people it takes to put something like this together including the trees that offer paper for us to be able to work with this information in physical form! On we go, my friends, let's go make some magic together and create a healthy world!

~ Jodie Harvala

I hope you have enjoyed this journey through the seasons, elements, and the moon. It has been a fabulous experience creating this course with Jodie; watching the workbook take form has been exhilarating! I have so much gratitude for what I've learned about myself in this process, how I enjoy creating and sharing, and more importantly helping others recognize how connected they are to the earth the stars. When you have a moment of clarity and witness a manifestation in your life that you created, you feel excited about life and all of the possibilities. My intention in my work is to help people remember the truth of who they are and get a little more comfortable walking through their fears. Each and every one of us is a powerful creator, no exceptions ... if you are in a body, you you are creating. Let's now do it with intention so we can thrive and love life more deeply.

~ Melissa Kim Corter

Other Products & Services By Melissa Kim Corter

*All of the following can be found on her website: www.melissacorter.com

Card deck: Nudges From Your Spirit
Weaved throughout this book you may have noticed pages with affirmative statements written on them. These statements are actual messages from the card deck, Nudges From Your Spirit. This deck contains 44 powerful messages for helping you connect with your own spirit.

E-Course: Nudges From Your Spirit
Want to explore this book and connect further with your own spirit? You can sign up for the e-course at any time. This course is 4-weeks long with the course materials sent directly to your inbox each week. It is filled with lessons, examples, stories, and audios for you to listen to. Once you go through it, then it is your to keep and revisit at any time!

Soul Artistry Portraiture Sessions
As a soul artist, Melissa loves to help her clients see themselves the way they deserve to be seen ... through the eyes and lens of love. Visit her website for more information and to read about how her transformational photo shoots can help you bring your vision to reality.

Nidra Meditations
Melissa has a special certification in Yoga Nidra, a form of meditation that she contributes to saving her own life. Yoga Nidra is for anyone who has a restless mind and spirit, cannot slow down their thoughts, and has some emotional healing they wish to support. This style of meditation is transformative and has helped people with anxiety, PTSD, addiction, trauma, depression, fear, stress, anger, and more. It is

unlimited in how it can help release patterns from the subconscious mind.

Seasons of Change- Invoking the Moon and the Magic of the Elements Course

This course is taught by Melissa Corter and Jodie Harvala; it's a fun way to learn about the seasons (solstices & equinoxes), the cycles of the moon, and the power of the four elements: earth, water, fire, and air. Each call is recorded and jam packed with information with a private Facebook support group.

Prosperity Intensive: Manifesting with Magic

This course is taught by Melissa Corter and Jodie Harvala. Shift how you attract and relate to prosperity. Lots of great insight and lessons to help you understand that it is the energy around money, prosperity, receiving, and deserving, not just money itself. Money has value because of the value we place upon it! You deserve to receive … join Jodie and Melissa and learn how to release the blocks to receiving.

The Empowerment Manual

In her chapter, "The Art of Self Awareness for Manifesting," Melissa provides you with five areas people become blocked in manifesting desired outcomes. Are you ready to stop responding to life circumstances and begin consciously creating them? Read her chapter in this powerful book and see how you can move past the illusion of the present moment and allow the magic to unfold.

You can also connect with Melissa here:

Art of Abundance: https://www.facebook.com/groups/artofabundance/

Melissa Corter- Soul Artist: https://www.facebook.com

www.melissacorter.com

OTHER PRODUCTS & SERVICES BY JODIE HARVALA

* All of the following can be found on her website: www.JodieHarvala.com

Card deck: The Wonderment Oracle Deck, ABC's of Intuition, ABC's of Affirmations

Each one of these decks creates a simple way to connect with spirit on a daily basis. Spirit loves to send signs and symbols as messages and all of these colorful decks create a connection and magical way to receive those messages.

E-Course: Time to be Brave, Transforming Anxiety

These courses are for those looking to dive a little deeper and actually clear the energy around different emotional parts of life that have a daily effect on how we live and walk through our life.

Space Clearing

As a psychic/medium, Jodie has a sense that tunes deeply into spaces and clearing energy can open up so many opportunities. Once the energy in your space is cleared you will notice so many things from getting off the couch and a new sense of motivation. Clearing spirits, emotions, trauma,and so much more. Create a space that supports you in every way.

Spirit School

For those looking to dig into intuition and how spirit works for you Jodie has created a online Spirit School! you can check out more details as well as a free video series at www.TheSpiritSchool.com

Seasons of Change- Invoking the Moon and the Magic of the Elements Course

This course is taught by Melissa Corter and Jodie Harvala; it's a fun way to learn about the seasons (solstices and equinoxes), the cycles of the moon, and the power of the four elements: earth, water, fire, and air. Each call is recorded and jam packed with information with a private Facebook support group.

Prosperity Intensive: Manifesting with Magic

This course is taught by Melissa Corter and Jodie Harvala. Shift how you attract and relate to prosperity. Lots of great insight and lessons to help you understand that it is the energy around money, prosperity, receiving, and deserving, not just money itself. Money has value because of the value we place upon it! You deserve to receive ... join Melissa and Jodie and learn how to release the blocks to receiving.

You can also connect with Jodie here:

https://www.facebook.com/jodie.harvala
www.JodieHarvala.com
www.TheSpiritSchool.com

RESOURCES

Moon Phases Astrology 2011, pg. 24

http://farmersalmanac.com/full-moon-names

Nolle, Richard. "Supermoon". Astropro (No publication date; modified March 10, 2011).

The Holy days information came from: https://carm.org/religious-movements/wicca/wiccan-sabbats-or-holy-days Major Sabbats

The Path of the Spiritual Sun written by Belsebuub & Angela Pritchard http://belsebuub.com/articles/the-spiritual-meaning-of-the-winter-solstice

https://en.wikipedia.org/wiki/Beltane

http://www.thewhitegoddess.co.uk/the_wheel_of_the_year/litha_-_summer_solstice.asp

http://www.thewhitegoddess.co.uk/the_wheel_of_the_year/lammas.asp

http://www.thewhitegoddess.co.uk/the_wheel_of_the_year/imbolc.asp

http://www.thewhitegoddess.co.uk/the_wheel_of_the_year/samhain.asp

http://www.spiritualresearchfoundation.org/spiritual-problems/effects-of-nature-and-environment/new-full-moon-effects/

NOTES

The Journey Continues...

Seasons of Change

4-Week Online Course
taught by
MELISSA CORTER and JODIE HARVALA

LEARN ABOUT:
- ☾ The seasons (Solstices & Equinoxes)
- ☾ The cycles of the moon
- ☾ The power of the four elements: earth, water, fire, and air
- ☾ 4 teleclasses–join us live or listen to the recordings
- ☾ Private Facebook Group!

Join us:
www.invokingmagic.com

www.ingramcontent.com/pod-product-compliance
Lightning Source LLC
Chambersburg PA
CBHW041659160426
43191CB00002B/30